T0347955

LGBTQI Digital Media Activism and Counter-Hate Speech in Italy

LGBTQI Digital Media Activism and Counter-Hate Speech in Italy analyzes the organizational communication practices of Italian LGBTQI activists.

The book investigates digital media activism practices, and how, through artifacts of political engagement, activists are championing social change through non-violent communications. The author also interrogates whether legal means are enough to combat hate and promote a culture of human rights.

This book is an essential read for students and scholars interested in LGBTQ rights and activism.

Sara Gabai has worked in Asia and Central Asia with European Union-funded programs, UN agencies, academic institutions, the private sector, NGOs, civil society organizations and local communities, on communication for development initiatives. Her passion and expertise range from human rights to digital media activism and freedom of expression, media literacy education, gender and women's economic empowerment, environmental and sustainability issues. Sara earned her PhD in Human Rights and Peace Studies (2021) from the Institute of Human Rights and Peace, Mahidol University, Thailand, an MSc in Gender, Media and Culture from the London School of Economics and Political Science (LSE), and a BA in Communications and a Minor in English Literature from John Cabot University, Italy.

Focus on Global Gender and Sexuality

The Poetry of Arab Women from the Pre-Islamic Age to Andalusia
Wessam Elmeligi

Interviews with Mexican Women
We Don't Talk About Feminism Here
Carlos M. Coria-Sanchez

Pornography, Indigeneity and Neocolonialism
Tim Gregory

Reading Iraqi Women's Novels in English Translation
Iraqi Women's Stories
Ruth Abou Rached

Gender Hierarchy of Masculinity and Femininity during the Chinese Cultural Revolution
Revolutionary Opera Films
Zhuying Li

Representations of Lethal Gender-Based Violence in Italy Between Journalism and Literature
Femminicidio Narratives
Nicoletta Mandolini

LGBTQI Digital Media Activism and Counter-Hate Speech in Italy
Sara Gabai

https://www.routledge.com/Focus-on-Global-Gender-and-Sexuality/book-series/FGGS

LGBTQI Digital Media Activism and Counter-Hate Speech in Italy

Sara Gabai

Routledge
Taylor & Francis Group

LONDON AND NEW YORK

First published 2022
by Routledge
4 Park Square, Milton Park, Abingdon, Oxon OX14 4RN

and by Routledge
605 Third Avenue, New York, NY 10158

Routledge is an imprint of the Taylor & Francis Group, an informa business

British Library Cataloguing-in-Publication Data
A catalogue record for this book is available from the British Library

Library of Congress Cataloging-in-Publication Data
A catalog record has been requested for this book

ISBN: 978-1-032-27054-8 (hbk)
ISBN: 978-1-032-27060-9 (pbk)
ISBN: 978-1-003-28995-1 (ebk)

DOI: 10.4324/9781003289951

Typeset in Times New Roman
by Taylor & Francis Books

Contents

Figures

Acknowledgments

The work that has been presented in this book would have not been possible without the continuous support of my mentors, who have stood by my side, near and far, all the steps of this journey. First and foremost, I want to thank Dr. Sriprapha Petcharamesree, who always encouraged me to take an intersectional approach to the study of human rights, peace, conflict and media, valuing my knowledge and strengths, and at the same time always pushing me to go further and beyond to expand these to other areas of research and inquiry. My gratitude also goes to Dr. Antonio López, who, over a decade ago, opened the doors to the fascinating world of media, communications and critical cultural studies, and whose teachings continue to inspire my everyday work and practice. I am also grateful to Dr. Lorenza Parisi, whose insights and knowledge of the LGBTQI social movement in Italy brought me closer to my roots, allowing me to conduct this research more confidently.

I have always been a strong believer that academic knowledge must necessarily inform resistance and activism on the ground. Our role as researchers, educators and activists is to bridge the gaps that exist at the intersection of theory and practice. Hence, this book is dedicated to all the representatives of Italian LGBTQI organizations who have taken part in this study and who have shared their knowledge and insights with me, driven by the shared and common commitment to raise awareness about those who are tirelessly working to advance a more emancipatory agenda for gender and human rights in Italy.

Thanks also to my family for always encouraging me to follow my dreams and passions, leading me to where I am today. Last, but not least, I want to express my gratitude to my partner M.T., who has always believed in my potential and supported me in every possible way at every step of this journey. This work would have not been possible without bringing into the process also our personal journeys of growth, love and commitment to advancing equality and justice.

1 Introduction

Setting the scene

The current population of Italy is 59,257,566 (ISTAT, 2021). There are approximately 1.6 million Italians who self-identify as lesbians, homosexuals or bisexuals (OECD, 2019), two million of whom declare they have engaged in a romantic or sexual relationship with a person of the same sex (ISTAT, 2012), and approximately 400,000 transgender people living in Italy, according to unofficial estimates based on the international scientific literature, explains Marina Pierdominici, researcher at the Istituto Superiore di Sanità (cited in Giangrande, 2020). The first official survey on the transgender population in Italy (called SPoT) was commissioned in 2020 by the University of Florence, the Istituto Superiore di Sanità, The Bridge Foundation, with the support of the National Observatory on Gender Identity. According to data released by the National Statistics Office (ISTAT, 2012) and Doxa-Amnesty International (2018), overall, the Italian population is aware of the lack of equal opportunities and discriminatory attitudes toward different social groups living on the national territory. Some 43.7 percent of the population consider women to be a target of discrimination, followed by immigrants (59.4 percent), homosexuals (61.3 percent) and transsexuals (80.3 percent) – these are the groups who are most at risk. Compared to heterosexuals, one citizen out of two strongly believes that homosexuals have less opportunities to find a job (49.6 percent) or to get promoted to higher positions (55 percent). One citizen out of five considers it unacceptable to have a homosexual colleague or supervisor; and that positions such as doctors, politicians and teachers should not be open to lesbian, gay, bisexual, trans, queer and intersex (LGBTQI) people. Moreover, even though the majority of the population does not consider homosexuality to be a disease, citizens still assume these are correlated, and that homosexuality is a synonym

DOI: 10.4324/9781003289951-1

for immorality, and a threat to traditional family relations and values. Some 41.4 percent of the population would not want a homosexual to be their neighbor, and among those who perceive homosexuality as a disease, 80 percent do not recognize LGBTQI people's right to get married (ISTAT, 2012).

The Italian legal system lacks statistics and case law on discrimination on the ground of sexual orientation and there is limited recognition of same sex partnerships among the population. The country is among the last in the European Union (EU) to adopt legislation recognizing same-sex unions, after decades of legal debate both in local courts and in the European Court of Human Rights. While on 20 May 2016, the Italian Chamber of Deputies approved the same-sex civil union bill, the Law 76/2016 was only passed after opponents introduced thousands of amendments and a provision for stepchild adoption was removed from the original bill. Problems persist even after the approval of this law as same-sex marriages performed abroad are not recognized in Italy. In a decision made in May 2018 by the country's Court of Cassation (Italy's highest court), an Italian and a Brazilian man who married in Brazil in 2012 were denied recognition of their marriage under Italian law. The supreme court judges agreed that the Italian law would recognize married same-sex couples only as civil partners, regardless whether they married before or after the introduction of the law on same-sex civil unions. According to the Italian-Brazilian couple, the ruling, which was the first of its kind since same-sex civil unions became legal, constituted discriminatory downgrading of their relationship status. Italy's refusal to legally recognize the marriages of same-sex couples married abroad violates the couple's rights to respect for private and family life, as ruled in December 2017 by the European Court of Human Rights for six other similar cases. Italian officials based the refusals to register these couples on an order issued by the Ministry of Internal Affairs on 26 March 2001 which affirmed same-sex marriage is "contrary to the norms of public order." While one Italian in two considers the law on civil unions' approval a step forward toward "a civilized society" (Doxa-Amnesty International, 2018), LGBTQI couples are still struggling for marriage equality. The strong influence of the Roman Catholic Church, conservative and religious actors who are collaborating nationally and transnationally on anti-gender campaigns and spreading discourse against LGBT rights, reproductive rights, surrogacy, sexual education, transgender rights, gender mainstreaming and antidiscrimination policies, are also still an obstacle to achieving equality.

In addition, the prevalence of discriminatory and homophobic language used by politicians and religious figures, and disseminated through both mainstream (national newspapers and television) and online social media (Facebook, Twitter and YouTube) cannot be ignored. It must be acknowledged that 41 million Italians are active on social media (Kemp, 2021), with Italy ranking sixth in Europe for its average daily social media use (Tankovska, 2021). The most popular platforms used by the population include YouTube (85.3 percent), WhatsApp (85.2 percent), Facebook (80.4 percent), Instagram (67 percent) and Twitter (32.8 percent) (Kemp, 2021). Several studies (Barretta and Milazzo, 2016; Ligas, 2011; Materassi, Tiezzi and Bencini, 2016; Scaramella, 2016) have also shown that uncontrolled and persistent use of sexist, racial, and xenophobic arguments, misinformation and incitement to violence against sexual minorities permeate media and political discourses, and spread like an oil spill through the Internet, particularly on Twitter, Facebook and YouTube channels. The Vox Observatory on Human Rights (2016) found homophobia to be the greatest indicator of intolerance online among the Italian population, particularly in the regions of Lombardia, Friuli, and Campania. The results were confirmed by the Eurobarometer Survey of the European Commission (2015), which showed that 73 percent of Italians believe that discrimination on the basis of sexual orientation is widespread in the country, as well as discrimination on the grounds of gender identity (71 percent). As much as the Internet and social media afford democratic participation by creating spaces where subordinate groups can participate in public deliberation and inform political and social change, one must not neglect the ways in which digital media are also being increasingly used as tools to oppress and persecute people.

Structural and cultural violence against sexual minorities in Italy greatly manifests itself through online hate speech, also called cyberhate. Even though there is no legally binding definition of the term "hate speech" in international law, and the topic has generated numerous debates among academics, media professionals, freedom of expression advocates, politicians, and lawyers, the most widely accepted definition of hate speech in Europe has been formulated by the European Commission against Racism and Intolerance (ECRI) in its General Policy Recommendation No. 15, adopted on 8 December 2015, as one that entails:

The use of one or more particular forms of expression – namely, the advocacy, promotion or incitement of the denigration, hatred or vilification of a person or group of persons, as well any harassment, insult, negative stereotyping, stigmatization or threat of such person or persons and any justification of all these forms of expression –that is based on a non-exhaustive list of personal characteristics or status that includes "race", color, language, religion or belief, nationality or national or ethnic origin, as well as descent, age, disability, sex, gender, gender identity and sexual orientation.

If it is true that online hate speech can indeed affect anyone, it is also true that LGBTQI people often experience abuse and harassment as a result of their gender, gender identity, sexual orientation, or sex characteristics (Reintke, 2016). According to 62 percent of human rights activists, social workers and members of the police from several countries in the EU who were interviewed by the EU Fundamental Rights Agency (EU FRA), sexual orientation and gender identity constitute the most prominent and severe reasons for verbal and physical aggression, after racism and xenophobia (EU FRA, 2013). Yet, as Materassi, Tiezzi and Bencini (2016) have argued, in Italy, there is still a lack of knowledge by police departments, and civil society in general, about what constitutes hate speech and hate crimes, discrimination, under-reporting, under-recording and racial profiling. Since it is still unclear how to denounce these offences and where to seek help, homophobic and transphobic hate crimes are particularly under-reported and LGBTQI victims are wiped from the public discourse. This trend is evident in the data on hate crime reporting presented by the Office for Democratic Institutions and Human Rights (ODIHR, 2015), where in 2015 alone, 42,379 cases of hate crimes were recorded by the police, the majority of which were against women, and only 45 cases were reported for crimes based on bias against LGBTQI people. Only one violent attack, the murder of a Brazilian transgender person, was reported by a civil society organization. According to more recent data from 2020, 1,111 cases of hate crimes were recorded, of which 71 were for crimes based on bias against LGBTQI people.

Methodological considerations

The way this research was conducted using different methodologies and approaches was driven by the author's strong commitment to interdisciplinary epistemology, one which binds researchers together not by agreement about answers but by shared commitments to questions. The motivation for choosing multi-site situational analysis, qualitative media analysis, multimodal critical discourse analysis and in-depth interviews with key experts from Italian LGBTQI organizations was driven by the strong belief that science and knowledge are rooted in narrative practices, metaphors and linguistic structures. Hence, the author has tried to think as much as possible across disciplinary boundaries (critical media and cultural studies, and human rights, peace and conflict studies) when theorizing, listening and analyzing across vectors of gender, sexuality, class, race and age. Social Movement Theory and Digital Media Activism are also important foundations for the theoretical and conceptual frameworks that have been developed in this research.

An extensive literature review was conducted to map out current national and international work on LGBTQI social movement mobilizations, digital media activism and advocacy, and whether good practices may be shared cross-culturally and scaled up. A multi-site situational analysis and the creation of interactive maps were used to collectively lay out Italian LGBTQI actors, identify their organizational communication and digital media activism practices, trace their geographic scope, networks and alliances, and the discourses and positions taken in their advocacy work. In conducting a qualitative media analysis and a multimodal critical discourse analysis of the websites and social media channels of selected organizations, it was evident that Facebook and Twitter were the most popular in organizations' communication work, hence the choice to focus and investigate further the use and contents shared through these two social media networks.

In the process of building actors' digital profiles, it was also important to identify the key thematic areas each organization is working on. To further verify the data collected through the multi-site situational analysis, a word cloud generator was used to create visual representations of the frequency of words included in organizations' statutes and mission statements. The analysis was strengthened through in-depth semi-structured interviews conducted with ten key experts working in organizations short-listed, based on their prominence and resonance on the Italian territory when promoting and protecting LGBTQI rights across key thematic areas. Multi-modal critical discourse analysis (Djonov and Zhao, 2014) and close readings of user-generated content were extremely important to understand the formal and informal strategies and tactics used in digital media activism. Critically analyzing different semiotic resources shed light on the ways in which activists resist or conform to dominant forms of culture and identity, or create oppositional meanings.

The structure of the book

This book is structured into seven chapters, including this Introduction and the Conclusion. We cannot fully understand social movements without understanding the dynamic relationship and interaction with their counterparts, hence, Chapter 2 presents an analysis of the emergence of the anti-gender countermovement in Europe and in Italy, its actors and networks, and the movement's intersection with specific political and religious projects. At the same time, when analyzing contemporary LGBTQI movement mobilizations and their organizational communication practices, one cannot overlook the history of the Gay and Lesbian Liberation Movement, and the media activism and cultural resistance practices that have arguably created the movement in the first place. Chapter 3 sheds light on the historical roots of LGBT mobilizations and the role media had in their formation.

The field of human rights rhetoric is still dominated by opposing views and debates on whether visualizing and communicating about human rights can improve the prospects of peace, justice, and democracy, or instead, legitimize, naturalize and perpetuate violence and injustice. In Chapter 4, the complex relationship between politics, human rights, and communications is explored, and in Chapter 5, a number of digital artifacts of political engagement of Italian LGBTQI actors are presented to showcase how activists are championing social change through non-violent communications. Chapter 6 then examines the effects of the implementation of Law 76/2016 on civil unions on the online discourses and attitudes of Italian publics prior to and after its enactment and assesses whether the law has been successful in promoting more favorable attitudes and behaviors toward the LGBTQI community. A reflection on whether legal means, including hate speech regulation, are enough to combat online and offline hate, attain justice and promote a culture of human rights and peace is also presented, particularly in the context of debates that have taken place in the months leading to the rejection of the Zan Bill against homotransphobia. Finally, Chapter 7 presents the conclusion.

References

Barretta, P. and Milazzo, G. (2016) Notizie oltre i muri: Quarto rapporto Carta di Roma, Available at: http://www.cartadiroma.org/wp-content/uploads/2016/12/Rapporto-2016_-cartadiroma.pdf.

Djonov, E. and Zhao, S. (2014) *Critical Multimodal Studies of Popular Discourse*, New York: Routledge.

Doxa-Amnesty International (2018) Indagine Doxa: per gli italiani discriminazioni ancora diffuse nel nostro paese. Available at: https://www.am nesty.it/indagine-doxa-gli-italiani-discriminazioni-ancora-diffuse-nel-nostro-paese/.

ECRI (2015) General Policy Recommendation No. 15 on Combating Hate Speech. Strasbourg: Council of Europe.

EU-FRA (European Union Agency for Fundamental Rights) (2013) European Union lesbian, gay, bisexual and transgender survey, Vienna: European Union Agency for Fundamental Rights.

European Commission (2015) Eurobarometer Survey: Discrimination in the EU in 2015. Available at: http://ec.europa.eu/COMMFrontOffice/publicopinion/index.cfm/Survey/getSurveyDetail/instruments/SPECIAL/surveyKy/2077.

Giangrande, A. (2020) *L'Italia Allo Specchio il DNA degli Italiani Anno 2020 Femmine e LGBTI Seconda Parte*. Independently published.

ISTAT (2012) La Popolazione omosessuale nella società Italiana, Rome: National Statistics Office. Available at: https://www.istat.it/it/files/2012/05/rep ort-omofobia_6giugno.pdf?title=Popolazione+omosessuale+nella+società+-+17%2Fmag%2F2012+-+Testo+integrale.pdf.

ISTAT (2021) Popolazione residente al 1 Gennaio. Available at: http://dati.istat.it/Index.aspx?DataSetCode=DCIS_POPRES1.

Kemp, S. (2021) Digital 2021: Italy. Available at: www.datareportal.com.

Ligas, A. (2011) Immigrazione, mass media e deontologia giornalistica, Rome: Carta di Roma. Available at: http://www.cartadiroma.org/wp-content/uploa ds/2015/10/Tesi-completa-.pdf.

Materassi, L., Tiezzi, M. and Bencini, C. (2016) L'odio non è un'opinione. Ricerca su hate speech, giornalismo, e migrazioni, EU Bricks Project. Available at: https://www.bricks-project.eu/wp/wp-content/uploads/2016/03/relazione_bricks_bassa.pdf.

ODIHR (Office for Democratic Institutions and Human Rights) (2015) Italy hate crime reporting. Available at: https://hatecrime.osce.org/italy?year=2015

OECD (2019) Society at a glance 2019. Available at: https://www.oecd-ilibrary.org/social-issues-migration-health/society-at-a-glance-2019_soc_glance-2019-en;jsessionid=oJA8PUxyp7Y9opuRdBUOzJLQ.ip-10-240-5-78.

Reintke, T. (2016) Report on gender equality and empowering women in the digital age, Brussels: Committee on Women's Rights and Gender Equality, European Parliament. Available at: https://www.giswatch.org/sites/default/files/gw2015-italy.pdf.

Scaramella, C. (2016) Discorsi d'odio e social media, Criticità, strategie e pratiche d'intervento, Fundamental Rights and Citizenship Program of the European Union. Available at: http://www.prismproject.eu/wp-content/uploads/2016/03/progetto-PRISM-ok-print-2.pdf.

Tankovska, H. (2021) Average daily social media use in selected European countries 2020, Statista. Available at: https://www.statista.com/statistics/719966/average-daily-social-media-use-in-selected-european-countries/.

Vox Observatory on Human Rights (2016) The maps of intolerance. Available at: http://www.voxdiritti.it/.

2 The anti-gender countermovement and the backlash against equality

If you know both yourself and your enemy, you can win a hundred battles without a single loss.

– Sun Tzu

Movement-countermovement dynamics: the emergence of the anti-gender countermovement in Europe

Scholars of contentious politics define a movement as "a group of actors who seek to change the legal and/or social status quo and a counter-movement as those who seek to preserve the status quo or to roll back recent changes to the status quo" (della Porta and Diani, 1999; Dorf and Tarrow, 2014; Meyer, Jenness, and Ingram, 2005; Tarrow, 2011; Tilly, 2004). In their analysis of anti-gender campaigns in Europe, Roman Kuhar and David Paternotte note that despite a diversity of triggers at national levels, anti-gender movements are transnationally connected and share common patterns of mobilization across borders, discourses, repertoires of action, strategies, frames and forms of organization. They can therefore be collectively defined as anti-gender in that all address gender ideology or "Gender Theory" as the root cause of the reforms they want to combat (Paternotte and Kuhar, 2018, p. 255). Most of these mobilizations started in 2010 in conjunction with specific policy debates and national reforms concerning lesbian, gay, bisexual, trans, queer and intersex (LGBTQI) rights, reproductive rights, marriage equality, sexual education, trans rights, gender studies, among others. In some countries, mobilizations were triggered by the refusal to ratify the Council of Europe Convention on preventing and combating violence against women and domestic violence (also known as the 2011 Istanbul Convention) or blocking the development of hate crime legislation to protect LGBTQI people.

DOI: 10.4324/9781003289951-2

Two main types of anti-gender mobilization can be identified in Europe. Those which have come together as a reaction to the proposal of new policies and which are in direct juxtaposition with LGBTQI actors, feminists and supporters of LGBTQI rights. The second kind of anti-gender mobilization uses a preventive model, by which even though new policies and reforms (marriage equality, for instance) have not yet been enacted nationally, protesters and lawmakers have come together to prevent the latter from emerging. This is the result of what Michael C. Dorf and Sidney Tarrow (2014) call the "anticipatory countermobilization" of a particular conservative or religious counter-movement prior to the determination of the LGBT community to mobilize on behalf of their fundamental human rights, including marriage equality. While same-sex marriage is legal in most of Western Europe, most countries in Central and Eastern Europe have taken a dramatically opposite stance to granting same-sex couples the right to marry.

In recent years, political homophobia and the number of constitutional bans on same-sex marriage have notably increased, with countries such as Georgia, Armenia, Slovakia, Croatia, and Hungary taking preventive action before LGBTQI activists could advocate for equality. Due to the severe repression of LGBTQI rights in post-communist countries, movements remained scattered and too weak to collectively respond to anticipatory countermobilizations. It must also be noted that the issue of same-sex unions was not even at the top of the movements' priority agenda since protection from discrimination, attaining social inclusion, combating hate crime and hate speech, among others, were more pressing issues (Mos, 2020). In most cases, the moral protectionist measures that were undertaken by conservative countries to preserve the traditional family institution hardly found their origins within the domestic context. In other words, it was not the country's civil society who demanded policy-makers adopt anti-LGBT policies or spearhead anti-gender initiatives. Constitutional bans on same-sex marriage likely resulted from "anticipatory homophobia" (ibid., p. 10), a precautionary measure to prevent the foreign wave of same-sex unions and the supranational organizations advocating for LGBTQI rights to interfere with national conceptualizations of the heterosexual family institution and its values. Following movement-countermovement dynamics, granting rights to LGBTQI people in Europe created a demand for conservative counteractions that ultimately resulted into an increase in constitutional bans on same-sex marriage, anti-LGBTI politics, and anti-gender mobilizations. While the response of conservative countries was distinct in each national context, the transnational dimension of the anti-gender movement allows us to identify a common logic (ibid.) that has been employed by actors as a backlash to restrain LGBTQI equality. This is one that involves:

- *The identification and construction of threat*: actors identify a threat to national security and family values (in this case, gender ideology/Gender Theory) and create narrative discourses against morally questionable alternatives. For instance, anti-LGBT conservative Catholic groups in Italy believe that homosexuality is a sin and an abomination that threatens to destroy the traditional natural family.
- *Threat attribution*: actors locate the origins of the threat abroad (often incarnated in supranational organizations or transnational LGBTQI rights defenders), outside the borders of the "pure" homeland. For instance, anti-LGBT activists in Italy believe in a conspiracy theory, according to which the United Nations, the Council of Europe, the European Parliament, and the World Health Organization are silently advancing the "Gender Diktat" or the "Dictatorship of Gender" in their global governance agenda (de Mattei, 2014).
- *Threat resolution*: through preventive measures (laws, policies and initiatives curtailing human rights), actors attempt to neutralize the foreign threat. In Italy, this has been most visible in the boycotting of gender studies and anti-discrimination programs in public schools, with conservative Catholic parents' organizations launching initiatives to monitor the spreading of "Gender Theory" and Gender Ideology.

In other instances, however, a reverse of this phenomenon took place; one in which the anti-gender movement became part of the political and legal opportunity structure for LGBTQI activists and allies, enabling a growing approval of LGBTQI issues even among those who were not directly interested in advocating for same-sex marriage, civil unions and LGBTQI rights. As Meyer explains, "Unfavorable changes in policy can spur mobilization, even at such times when mobilization is unlikely to have much noticeable effect on policy" (2004, p. 137). This was the case in Italy, where, by lobbying against the recognition of same-sex civil unions, the anti-gender movement paved the way for a more intersectional, unified and collective LGBTQI Italian movement. As Lavizzari points out, not only did the "anti-gender mobilization push the LGBTIQ movement toward a reconfiguration of internal voices and the identification of a common enemy" (2020, p. 145), it also pushed activists to build alliances and networks with other movements beyond the LGBTQI community, strengthening their legitimacy and recognition.

The Italian anti-gender movement: the intersection of religion, politics and activism

The Catholic Church has played a critical role in the emergence and the development of gender ideology and anti-gender movements. Several scholars (Doris Buss, 1988; 2004; Mary Anne Case, 2011, 2016; Bracke and Paternotte, 2016) trace the emergence of the notion of gender ideology or "Theory of Gender"[1] to debates taking place at the Vatican in the aftermath of two remarkable historical events. The United Nations International Conference on Population and Development (ICPD) in Cairo in 1994, where a 20-year Program of Action was adopted by 179 governments, one that recognized sexual and reproductive health and the empowerment of women and girls as fundamental human rights and a cornerstone to development and population concerns. The second event was the Fourth World Conference on Women in Beijing (1995), where 189 countries unanimously adopted the Beijing Declaration and the Platform for Action, still considered today the key policy framework on gender equality and the human rights of women and girls. The Church feared that sexual and reproductive rights would internationally justify abortion, redefine notions of motherhood and the natural family and legitimize homosexuality and "deviant" behavior. This is in a context where the Treaty of Amsterdam (1997), which came into force on 1 May 1999, officially recognized for the first time in a Treaty, discrimination on the grounds of sexual orientation (Article 13), and in 2001, the Netherlands became the first country in Europe to legalize same-sex marriage. Arguably, since the first ICPD Conference, the same fears and claims for "morality" have led to an increasing direct or indirect criminalization of sexuality and reproduction by governments all around the world (Amnesty International, 2018). The misuse of criminal law, restrictive regulations and denial of sexual and reproductive rights often negatively impact the health and violate the human rights of people, perpetuate inequality, and place women, girls and LGBTQI people at greater risk of discrimination, marginalization, and gender-based violence. Individuals who support states and their justifications to criminalize sexuality and reproduction are those conservative actors also taking part in anti-gender mobilizations.

Semantic battle: the Vatican's response to reclaiming the discourse on gender

The Italian anti-gender countermovement cannot be fully studied without first investigating its intersection with specific religious and political projects, in particular, recognizing the critical role that the Vatican and religious groups have played in the emergence and the development of gender ideology and "Gender Theory." Most anti-gender mobilizations started in conjunction with specific policy debates and national reforms concerning LGBTQI rights, reproductive rights, marriage equality, sexual education, trans rights, gender studies, among others. In Italy, among the main actors in the political arena debating on these issues were conservative religious groups that not only exercised great political and electoral power, influencing policy-making, but also played a critical role in defining the language spoken by anti-gender movements worldwide, one deeply infused in misleading concepts such as "gender ideology" and "Theory of Gender." As Garbagnoli explains:

> Paradoxically, gender has started to exist as an efficient political category thanks to the Vatican. It was not only appropriated by protestors in the terms constructed by the Vatican – a hotchpotch mixing and distorting different feminist and queer theories and claims – but it was also re-signified as the symbol of what these conservative actors regarded as abnormal and anti-national in the contemporary Italian context.
>
> (2017, p. 151)

Several Catholic scriptures and publications became the prelude to how we (mis)understand gender in contemporary Italy and the rest of the world.

Pope John Paul II's *Theology of the Body* (1979–1984), which outlines the difference and complementarity of the sexes, and the *Compendium of the Social Doctrine of the Church* published by the Pontifical Council for Justice and Peace in 2004, at the request of John Paul II, were key in the construction of the discourse on gender ideology. In the latter document, the Church not only positions itself as "an expert in humanity" (ibid., p. 61), but also re-emphasizes the hetero-normative true meaning of sexuality, one on which "marriage, the flourishing of family life and the harmony of the couple and society depend" (ibid., p. 224). The text also expresses concerns about the ways personal sexual identity has come to be viewed as an outcome of cultural and social conditioning:

Faced with theories that consider gender identity as merely the cultural and social product of the interaction between the community and the individual, independent of personal sexual identity without any reference to the true meaning of sexuality, ... it is obligatory that positive law be conformed to the natural law, according to which sexual identity is indispensable, because it is the objective condition for forming a couple in marriage.

(ibid., p. 224)

Any possibility of self-realization through one's own identity and of legal recognition of non-heteronormative partnerships is excluded in the Catholic discourse of these two texts.

However, the publication that has most notably contributed to the creation of the semantics of anti-gender discourse and the definition of the "Theory of Gender" is the *Lexicon: Ambiguous and Debatable Terms Regarding Family Life and Ethical Questions* (Pontifical Council for the Family, 2003). Published in 2003 by the former Pontifical Council for the Family, this glossary of 78 terms on bioethics, sexuality and family, was the Vatican's response to the supposedly ambiguous and hijacked "dominant discourse" used during the Beijing Conference to promote causes often at odds with the Catholic moral understanding. The *Lexicon* project is important in the context of anti-gender mobilizations in that, as Corredor explains, it was the Catholic counter-response in order to:

Refute claims concerning the hierarchical construction of the gendered and heterosexual order; essentialize and delegitimize feminist and queer theories of gender; frustrate global and local gender mainstreaming efforts; thwart gender and LGBTQI equality policies; and finally, reaffirm heteropatriarchal conceptions of sex, gender, and sexuality.

(2019, p. 616)

This is reflected in the language and discourses used in dedicated chapters on *Bioethics, Dignity of the Human Embryo, New Family Models, Dangers of the Ideology of Gender, Homosexuality and Homophobia, Homosexual "Marriage", Sexual Identity and Difference, Sexual and Reproductive Health, Sexual Identity and Difference*, which constitute the Vatican's rhetoric on the matter of gender, one that will become instrumental for the political mobilization of contemporary anti-gender movements and their discriminatory discourses.

In Italy, anti-gender mobilizations have specifically targeted the *Scalfarotto Bill* (2013) against discrimination on the ground of sexual orientation and gender identity, the *Cirinnà Bill* (2013) on the recognition of same-sex civil unions, and the *Fedeli Bill* (2014) on the inclusion of gender studies in schools and universities. As Corredor maintains: "Anti-genderism is first and foremost an epistemological response to emancipatory claims about sex, gender, and sexuality, and second, a political mechanism used to contain policy developments associated with feminist and queer agendas" (ibid., p. 614).

The years-long discussions that led to the adoption of the Cirinnà Bill on civil unions were the launching pad and a turning point for anti-gender mobilizations in Italy. On 12 May 2007, during the first Family Day, a rally organized in Rome by the Catholic Forum of Family Associations to counter the *DICO Bill* on civil unions, the term "gender" was never mentioned by activists; yet, anti-gender discourse was already permeating in the public arena. Alfonso Cardinal López Trujillo, author of the *Lexicon*'s Preface, had earlier warned against the misleading and deliberate use of the word "families" (in the plural form) by the United Nations during the celebration of the International Year of the Family. For the Cardinal, this was a move on behalf of the UN to reject the natural institution of the family and undermine the certainty of its future (Pontifical Council for the Family, 2003, p. xviii). Similarly, Professor Aquilino Polaino-Lorente attacked pioneer countries like Denmark, Norway, Sweden, the Netherlands and Spain for legalizing same-sex marriage, and declared their decision demonstrated that a profound disorder was in place in these countries. According to Polaino-Lorente:

> To recognize the capacity of homosexuals to unite in marriage presupposes an acceptance of the 'new state of things'. These relations cannot be made equivalent, simply because of the fact of the type of union between homosexuals cannot be considered equal or equivalent to the martial union between a man and a woman.
>
> (ibid., p. 453)

Hence, since no other family models can exist following this myopic view, there is no validity in using terms like "single-parent families," "de facto unions," "love couples," "permanent affective unions," "extended family," among others. These and many other discriminatory and exclusionary discourses related to the family and marriage are thoroughly fleshed out in the *Lexicon*, where clear calls to action on how to resist the "new state of things" are also being proposed. Ultimately, in 2012, the term "Family Day" officially entered the *Treccani Encyclopedia* to define the "day dedicated to the defense of traditional family values, generally promoted by Catholic-inspired movements, as opposed to demonstrations in favor of the legal recognition of homosexual families" (Treccani Instituto, 2012). It is important to understand that what is at stake in the semantic battle to institutionalize the discourse on gender is the power to privilege certain epistemological standpoints (sexist, homophobic, racist, xenophobic, capitalist, patriarchal, classist, white, and so on) and define and validate the moral parameters within which humanity is expected to abide. Recognizing policies promoting reproductive rights, gender as a social and cultural construct, the multiplicity of sexes, equal citizenship rights for gender and sexual orientations, would not only subvert the Catholic Church's gender essentialism reflected in its religious doctrines, but also undermine its political influence in shaping language, culture, society, identities and subjectivities.

Actors, networks and alliances in Italy's anti-gender mobilizations

In the years leading up to the adoption of the Cirinnà Law on civil unions, offline and online mobilizations to #StopGender have sprung up like mushrooms, with social media becoming key locations of action-shaping mobilization, recruitment, membership and participation in the movement. Conferences and public meetings on "Gender Theory" and gender ideology were regularly organized in partnership with public institutions all over the national territory, strengthening and legitimizing the main anti-gender discourse. Public demonstrations embodied by the Standing Sentinels, an anti-gender group, also took place in hundreds of Italian public squares and became the arena for anti-gender protesters to voice their discourses on "normalized" sexuality, acceptable biological behavior and gender norms. During these events, homophobia and hate speech against LGBTQI people were on the rise, with slogans reading "NO Gender, Let's save our children's childhood," "Beware of fake families. Protect the family. NO to gay marriage," "Say NO more Gay, Enough Faggots," to name just a few. The rising homophobia has also been reported by the Vox Observatory on Human Rights in its map of intolerance (2016), where, by analyzing discourses proliferating on Twitter between August 2015 and February 2016, homophobic discourse was found to be the most prominent, followed by antisemitism, racism, disability, misogyny and islamophobia. Rome, Milan, Naples and Bologna were identified as the most homophobic cities in Italy. Interestingly, when comparing the results of the first map (prior to the enactment of the civil unions law), with the map of intolerance issued in 2019, it is evident that during the period of March–May 2019, the dissemination of homophobic discourse on Twitter has decreased (with antisemitism now ranking top). While the majority of Italians now believe that LGBTQI people should enjoy equal rights, the incidence of hate is far from being over. Homophobic attacks are most visible (both online and offline) especially during debates on rainbow families (those families where a child or several children have at least one parent who identifies as LGBTQI) or concomitant with events led by anti-abortion, anti-feminist, and anti-LGBTQI movements, such as the 13th International Conference of the World Congress of Families (WCF) which took place in Verona in 2019 (Vox Observatory on Human Rights, 2019).

Actors and networks involved in anti-gender mobilizations are analyzed in this book in order to understand the ideological matrix of these mobilizations, their tactics and repertories of action, and their intersection with populist right and neo-fascist political projects. During the spring of 2013, the Italian anti-gender movement began to take shape following the footsteps of the French Collective La Manif pour Tous (Demonstration for All). As Lavizzari (2020) notes, its organizational structure is characterized by a relatively small number of powerful individual players; strong links between activists and local, social and religious realities which are key for recruitment at the grassroots level; and the establishment of a flexible and non-binding affiliation model that has enabled the movement's network to rapidly expand across the national territory. Finally, direct access to positions of power, particularly in the political and religious arenas, and strong ties with the Opus Dei and the Italian Episcopal Conference (CEI), have contributed to the movement's funding and institutionalization. A varied number of actors and allies, some being more established than others, mobilize the anti-gender movement. A shared system of values and beliefs rooted in Catholic doctrinal principles is used to recruit individuals who, once in the movement, move across a spectrum of religious values, expressing their faith in terms of pro-family, pro-life and anti-gender values.

Leading groups in the anti-gender movement include:

- Giuristi per la Vita (Jurists for Life);
- Forum delle Famiglie (Families Forum);
- Scienza and Vita (Science and Life);
- Notizie Pro Vita and Famiglia (News Pro-Life and Family);

- Azione Cattolica (Catholic Action);
- Alleanza Cattolica (Catholic Alliance);
- Famiglia Domani (Tomorrow's Family);
- Comitato Difendiamo I Nostri Figli – CDNF (Committee to Defend Our Children);
- Sentinelle in Piedi (Standing Sentinels);
- La Manif pour Tous Italia – Generazione Famiglia (LMPTI).

Paternotte and Kuhar (2018) cluster these actors in at least three categories (Figure 2.1): the first, encompassing members of anti-abortion groups, Catholic organizations and political parties who existed before the emergence of the movement and who have used gender ideology to relaunch their activism. The second, constituting newly established associations, initiatives and groups such as the La Manif pour Tous Italia, the Standing Sentinels, the Committee to Defend Our Children (main organizer of the Family Day), which were specifically created to counteract gender ideology and to unite and mobilize pre-established organizations under one umbrella during anti-gender campaigns. These actors also represent the "brand identity" of the movement due to their wide access to mainstream media and social media and a strong voice in decision-making processes. The third actors are allies or bystanders of the movement (politicians, media professionals, influencers, teachers and academics from pontifical universities, doctors, lawyers, parents, among others), who interact with other groups to a different extent. While protesters often identify as being apolitical, many associations have direct access to public offices and politics.

At the front of the Italian anti-gender mobilization is La Manif pour Tous Italia (LMPTI), which unlike the French collective, is an association that soon became the point of reference for a wide range of protesters and allies (in Italy and Europe), uniting both nationally and

Figure 2.1 Main actors in the Italian anti-gender movement based on Paternotte and Kuhar's (2018) categories

transnationally main Catholic family associations and traditional far-right movements. LMPTI operates mainly through online networks using disparate strategies and tools to reach out to actors, share initiatives launched by associations and mobilize action online and offline. While LMPTI appears to encompass a vast network of actors and committees, in reality, as De Guerre points out, "such committees are interconnected empty containers relying on the same few anti-gender actors, who often belong to already existing anti-abortion associations" (2015–2016). Radical, well-established anti-abortion groups such as Science and Life, Jurists for Life and News Pro-Life and Family are among the most powerful militants who have taken the gender movement as a political opportunity to reinvigorate their activism and bring anti-abortion discourse back into the public arena. Established in 2004 with the support of the Italian Episcopal Conference (CEI), Science and Life became the Vatican's greatest supporter in the battle to stop the referendum on assisted reproductive technology. Moreover, the transnational character of anti-gender mobilizations is reflected in the work of the Jurists for Life, the Pro-Life and Family News, and the Standing Sentinels, which act as the Italian focal points for international and oversees anti-abortion, anti-LGBTQ groups, and radical right neo-fascist political groups such as Forza Nuova and Casa Pound Italia (Bianchi, 2017). The latter are known for engaging in direct violent confrontation with members of the LGBTIQ movement during public demonstrations.

Tactics and strategies of anti-gender actors

While the Italian anti-gender movement encompasses a variety of different actors, who also forge alliances with external players (for instance, from the political, religious, medical, and educational arenas), its tactics and strategies are distinctive and an expression of the movement's ideas, culture and traditions. This section will address the main tactics and strategies used by actors in the anti-gender movement to appropriate spaces and articulate their collective interests, claims and targets. The literature of scholars of anti-gender mobilizations in Italy (Garbagnoli, 2017; Garbagnoli and Prearo, 2018; Lavizzari, 2020; Prearo, 2020) shows a consistency in actors' tactical repertoires of action. These include:

1   The organization of events, conferences and public meetings on "The Theory of Gender" and gender ideology – to create closer links between anti-gender actors across geographical and religious lines and strengthen political discourse.

2   Public demonstrations and eventful protests – to strengthen the movement's unity and branding, reinforce anti-gender discourses, and gain support of public administrations on anti-gender measures.
3   Online networking and digital media activism, expressed through social media campaigns – to spread anti-gender rhetoric, raise funds, and advertise activities.

Several cases will also be presented to assess the impact of the tactics and strategies used, in particular in the context of the highly contested World Congress of Families (WCF) that took place in Verona, Italy, in 2019.

Social mobilization through events, conferences and public meetings

Since the beginning of anti-gender mobilizations, hundreds of conferences, public meetings and gatherings have been organized on the national territory to carefully craft the narrative discourse on gender. Most often, distorted notions of gender have been appropriated by the movement's orators and key influencers to bring forward a very clear anti-democratic political agenda in defense of nature, the nation and normality (Paternotte and Kuhar, 2018). While these conferences and public events are promoted by their organizers as apolitical venues for scientific and educational knowledge exchange, in reality, these are true political rallies aimed to recruit followers in anti-gender countermobilizations, particularly, those led by anti-abortionist, pro-life movements and anti-LGBTQI groups. The 13th International Conference of the World Congress of Families (WCF) which took place in Verona, Italy, on 29–31 March 2019 under the disputed patronage of the Presidency of the Council of Ministers, Minister of Family and Disability (the logo of the former was later deleted), is worth of analysis in that the high profile international event was both the platform for introducing to an international audience the Italian anti-gender countermovement and its new consolidated organizational structure, and the space for strengthening transnational anti-gender networks, and reaffirming the countermovement's legitimacy in religious and political arenas (Prearo, 2020). The WCF can be considered the quintessential tactic of transnational anti-gender events mobilization and a key site for political right-wing strategies' development and dissemination. With congresses organized since the mid-1990s in Prague (1997), Geneva (1999), Mexico City (2004), Warsaw (2007), Amsterdam (2009), Madrid (2012), Sydney (2013), and Moscow (2014), the WCF has become an annual event in the years of rising anti-gender mobilizations in Europe and worldwide:

Using a deceptive pro-family rhetoric, WCF's campaign for the 'natural family' is being used to promote new laws justifying the criminalization of LGBTQ people and abortion, effectively unleashing a torrent of destructive anti-choice and anti-LGBTQ legislation, persecution, and violence around the world that ultimately damages—and seeks to dismantle—any and all 'nontraditional' families.

(Parke, 2017)

This is clearly visible in alliances forged by Brian Brown, President of the Congress of Families, and Allan Carlson, Founder and International Secretary, with the French La Manif Pour Tous, or through their support for Russia's "Gay Propaganda Law," one that greatly contributed to the rise of stigma, harassment and violence against LGBTQI people. In the context of Italy, the WCF has worked closely with anti-LGBTQI actors in the five years prior to the Congress, including with Generazione Famiglia (Family Generation), Comitato Difendiamo I Nostri Figli (Committee to Defend Our Children), and ProVita (Pro-Life), conducting several training workshops on how to effectively lobby against legislation recognizing LGBT rights, reproductive rights, gender studies, and even immigration. In the political arena, Brown has established strong alliances with Matteo Salvini, former Deputy Prime Minister of Italy and defender of the "natural family," as well as far-right Catholic Lorenzo Fontana, former Minister for Families and Disabilities, Marco Busetti, former Minister of Education, and actors involved in the organization of the "Family Day," such as senator Simone Pillon (also one of the main opponents of the Zan Bill) and Massimo Gandolfini. These and other political actors from right political parties attended the Congress in Verona.

The WCF, which was enlisted by the Southern Poverty Law Center as an anti-LGBT hate group, also played a critical role in redefining the linguistics and communication strategies of anti-gender mobilizations and setting key priority issues on their militant agenda. As Prearo (2020) maintains, the Congress functioned as a lab for the production of ideologies, values and plans on life, gender, sexuality, and family; a space in which the languages of Catholic doctrines and Vatican texts were being adapted and translated into a more scientific, philosophical, historical and anthropologic language, one that was practical and ready for political use. Key priorities shifted throughout the years. Until 2013, the pro-life rhetoric dominated the language of Italian mobilizations, it then switched to anti-gender discourse until 2016, finally, the rhetoric to defend the natural family and traditional family values has become the epicenter of the movement (Figure 2.2).

The communications strategy adopted by actors has also undergone a change. Positive tones and references to the theme of love and beauty, the protection of human rights and the identification of heroes are replacing sensational and violent anti-abortionist communications. As Claudia Torrisi, freelance journalist for Valigia Blue, VICE Italy, and Open Democracy notes:

> It is now rare to find the classical image of the fetus in narrative discourses and visual representations. The rhetoric, the lexical, and the campaigns of the WCF and its affiliated groups are more similar to those spearheaded by groups who work in favor of human rights and feminist movements.
>
> (*Il Post*, 2019)

This is a strategy used to legitimize discourses that instead conceal racist or sexist ideologies.

The promotional video of the Verona World Congress of Families entitled "Never Stop Being Amazed" is a great example of the change in communication strategy and the frames that are being used in the "family" discourse promoted by anti-gender actors. As the piano starts playing, the voice of a white male narrator advancing toward the camera addresses the audience with the questions: "Do you know how many million forms of life exist on this planet? How many billion galaxies exist above our heads?" The "narrator-scientist" then provides statistics to support the fact that our world is one that bursts with life. He warns, however, that life is not to be taken for granted. A reference to Erwin Schrödinger, the 1933 Nobel Prize-winner for Physics, is made. We are the result of an unlikely statistic and to be present on this planet, privileged conditions are necessary. The main biological

2013   **2016**   **2020**

Pro-life	Anti-gender	Natural Family
Anti-Abortion	Gender Theory	Traditional Values
	Gender Ideology	Rights of the Child

Figure 2.2 Changes in discourse of pro-life and anti-gender groups (2013–2020)

components to exist in this world are: carbon, hydrogen, nitrogen, oxygen, phosphorous, sulfur and water. Looking through the glass of a window facing nature, the thoughtful "narrator-scientist" then discovers there is something lacking among these components. "We need energy." In a change of scene, directly facing the camera, the narrator reinstates, "A primordial energy – LOVE," followed by a scene of two hands holding in the sky (a male and a female with a wedding ring). The "narrator-scientist" continues to explain:

> The ability to reproduce new beings similar to us is one of the most complex autocatalytic reactions we know. This is what forges family. The union between a man and a woman generates new life. So, the family becomes the quintessence of the universe's creative expansion.

Amazed by the miracle of life, he affirms, "Come on, it's awesome. Tell me if all this beauty should not be cherished" (the scene switches to a family with two boys running outdoors in nature). The narrator then picks up a Polaroid photo of Chiara Corbella, seen by many Catholics as a "Servant of God." Diagnosed with cancer, Chiara died aged 28 years old because she rejected any treatment during her pregnancy. He adds, "In her disarming simplicity she understood it well, 'Life, what a miracle, my love!'." Another Polaroid photo is shown, this time portraying English writer, philosopher, and lay theologian G.K. Chesterton and his quote "The world will never starve for want of wonders, But only for want of wonder." As the camera zooms into the face of the narrator, the video is about to conclude with the heroic narrative discourse. "The Hero is who sparks hope in the world, and the world is in need of heroes." A sequence of more Polaroid photos representing "cultural" heroes runs in front of the camera. In the closing scene, the narrator invites the audience to come to Verona and participate in the World Congress on Families. The final message he delivers is: "Never Stop Being Amazed!". A graphic logo of two joined halves of one heart (blue and pink, symbolizing the love between a man and a woman) ends the video.

This promotional video clearly shows sometimes more overtly, sometimes covertly, the changes in narrative discourse and visual representations spearheaded by pro-life and anti-abortion activists. Anti-gender actors have arguably become more sophisticated in using digital media and marketing tools to intellectualize and give authority to their conservative and regressive interpretations of culture, religion and tradition. As shown in this video example from the Verona World

Congress of Families, sensational and violent anti-abortionist communications have been replaced by positive tones and references to the
theme of love and beauty, the protection of human rights and the
identification of heroes.

Public demonstrations and eventful protests

Protests are one of the main repertoires of action of social movements.
The Standing Sentinels and their spontaneous gatherings in major
squares on the national territory, or the mobilizations that took place
during Family Day events and Marches for Life, embody the wave of
anti-gender demonstrations and protests targeted against the Scalfarotto Bill (2013), against discrimination on the ground of sexual orientation and gender identity, the Cirinnà Bill (2013), on the recognition
of same-sex civil unions, and the Fedeli Bill (2014), on the inclusion of
gender studies in schools and universities. Carefully staged through
coordinated behavior during stand-ins and sit-ins, the organization of
colorful parades (pink for mom, blue for dad), and an alignment in
choirs and chants and violent discriminatory messages and slogans,
these protests were key to strengthening the movement's unity and
branding, reinforcing anti-gender discourses, and gaining the support
of public administrations on anti-gender measures. Once again, one
cannot ignore the transnational dimension of these public demonstrations and protests, and their strong alliances with powerful networks in
Europe, the United States, and the rest of the world. This is the case of
the well-established March for Life, which as Virginia Coda Nunziante,
one of the first organizers of the March in Italy has claimed, was fully
inspired and organized following the model of the march that takes
place annually in Washington, DC (Zenit.org, 2012).

With circa 10,000 people gathered in Verona, the March for Life
(also termed by others the March for Family) that took place on 31
March 2019, was the closing event of the WCF and a case worth analyzing in order to shed light on the interconnectedness of actors, networks and repertoires of action involved in the organization of protests
and public demonstrations in Italy. Key actors involved in the organization of this March were not surprisingly also those involved in the
organization of the WCF, including established pro-life organizations
and Catholic groups. The proximity and interconnectedness of the
WCF and the March for Life allow us to frame this form of protest as
what Donatella della Porta (2008) has called an eventful protest with
transformative effects; one in which, "networking in action" is pivotal
to increasing the influence of each organization and individuals, and

empowering them in new ways. In Verona, the networking logic of the March not only has strengthened the collective identity of the movement, but also has created the conditions for collective action. Brian Brown's short opening message delivered on stage hints to the relevance of the transnational dimension of the movement:

> Brothers and sisters, what a day to be in the beautiful city of Verona, standing for the Family. I come from the United States to say you are not alone! Throughout the world people are standing up to say the family is worth defending.
>
> (March for Life, 2019)

The networking and bonds that are being built between actors and protesters throughout the duration of these events (not just counterparts in the United States, but also those in Russia, Hungary, Poland, among other conservative countries) play a critical role in the process of strengthening protesters' motivation and emotions, nourishing solidarity and a sense of belonging, and informing political action.

In the age of global and digital media, eventful protests have also become the space where common spectacles are being staged. With hired professional videographers and photographers standing on the Verona Arena in Piazza Bra overlooking the stage and the crowd from above, and others positioned on the ground, this March for Life is a true *media spectacle* (Kellner, 2012). In other words, a technologically mediated event carefully constructed to raise its visibility and present to a wider online audience the movement's identity, culture, political stance and claims. The video of the March for Life fully captures the staging and performative process in action. The main camera initially pans out to the crowd showing the people who have gathered in the public square (families, children, elderly people, youths). It then turns to the center of the stage, where a series of remarks are being delivered by all white male event organizers and allies, including Brian Brown and Alexey Komov, Honorary President of the Lombardia-Russia Association and Ambassador of the WCF in Russia. The younger presenter (same narrator of the video promo), who throughout the delivery of these remarks has stood mainly in the background, shadowed by the leading actors, subsequently advances toward the center of the stage and starts directing the performance. He explains to the crowd how they should record their testimony: "Let's all turn around toward the Arena"; "Say ciao to the two men in white shirts standing on top of the Arena" (the photographer and videographer); "Say Viva la Famiglia" (Long live the Family); "Great, now march slowly slowly and in an organized manner." The media spectacle is most visibly captured in the next words spoken by the presenter:

> Let's simply communicate our testimony in an authentic manner, by being our true selves; not in a fake manner ... as I have suggested earlier and I will repeat it again now, take your phones out, good, not so much to capture photos here on site. Let's provide our testimony, hug each other, be visible not only through your march, but also through your online testimony, now being online is a part [of protest strategies].

From the video it is clear that most protesters feel uneasy hugging strangers, with one woman even stating "we hug spiritually." Moreover, it is evident that particularly senior citizens and children are not familiar with the use and value of social media advocacy strategies. As opposed to smartphones, protestors are expressing their activism by carrying statues of the Virgin Mary, photos of Jesus, the Saints and the Pope, proudly displaying their crucifix in front of the main camera, and carrying pro-family banners and posters. The use and repetition of the word "testimony" are significant for the media spectacle – in this instance, the word has been fully expropriated of its value and meaning (for instance, the power of testimony in the context of transitional justice), and instead is purely being used by the presenter as a marketing strategy to increase the visibility of the movement on social media. No substantial "call to action" has been made to trigger protesters to more actively take part in digital media activism and social media campaigning. On the other hand, for the first time since the establishment of the first WCF in 1997, more than 30,000 protesters from Italy and Europe launched a counter-response and took over Verona. The demonstration was led by the *Non Una di Meno* feminist group (inspired by the Argentinian movement *Ni Una Menos*) and affiliated national and international organizations.

Online networking and digital media activism

The anti-gender movement has certainly leveraged the potential of digital media and social networks to organize its mobilization, recruit followers, strengthen networks both nationally and transnationally, and widely disseminate information across multiple media channels. Many organizations and associations involved in this movement often have their own official websites, blogs, Facebook pages, and mailing lists, connecting and cross-sharing each other's contents. As Lavizzari (2020, p. 61) explains: "Each group acts as a mouthpiece, as a sounding board, for the positions or actions of the other, generating a growing network of activists to consolidate and expand the foundations of the movement's social base." Popular online strategies used by actors include basic forms of hacktivism such as automated email bombs sent to politicians to protest government policies (this could potentially jam a recipient's inbox, making it hard for other emails to get through), extensive use of online media as a battlefield for spreading anti-gender discourse, hate speech, and counteracting narratives pro-LGBTQI, the creation of Facebook groups and events (also linked to public demonstrations), the use of social media for networking and organizing, creating boycott campaigns, launching online petitions, among others.

CitizenGo, the world's main "profamily" and "pro-life" platform is a good example to analyze when showing the global resonance of this networked infrastructure of influence operating both online and in real-life tangible spaces. With a membership of more than 16 million people (as of 2021), CitizenGo describes itself as: "A community of active citizens who work together, using online petitions and action alerts to defend and promote life, family and liberty, and ensure that those in power respect human dignity and individuals' rights" (2020). In reality, the organization is best known for coordinating large-scale online petitions and collecting signatures against same-sex marriage, against abortionist legislation, against the "imposition of gender ideology" in schools, and against persecution of Christians by Islamism in Asia and Africa. Among the most renowned campaigns led in Italy are the CitizenGo orange "hate buses" across cities, advertising slogans against LGBTQI rights and "feminazi" and the Stop Abortion Campaign #stopaborto. The latter was launched on 22 May 2018, a date that marked the 40th anniversary of Law 194, which came into force in May 1978, and which guarantees the right to terminate a pregnancy during the first 90 days when continuing the pregnancy would pose a threat to the physical or mental health of the woman. CitizenGo printed posters and set up billboards across the city of Rome with slogans reading "Abortion. Prime cause of feminicide in the world." The campaign was ultimately censured by the Municipality of Rome, with CitizenGo announcing a new campaign under the same hashtag #stopaborto, this time launched on 17 May, on the occasion of the International Day Against Homophobia. According to Filippo Savarese, former CitizenGo Campaign Director, the censorship was an unprecedented attack on the freedom of expression of life defenders (*Roma*

Today, 2018). The organization furthermore invited people to express their dissent by joining the March for Life that took place just two days later, on 19 May.

With headquarters in Madrid and team members scattered in 15 cities in three continents, among the Foundation's Board of Trustees are: Ignacio Arsuaga, President and Founder of CitizenGo (also one of the main organizers of Verona WCF), Brian Brown, President of the WCF, and Luca Volontè, Italian politician and former Chair of the European People's Party (EPP) in the Council of Europe, also a member of the WCF. Paternotte and Kuhar (2016) have defined these actors as "transnational brokers" and the most active figures in spreading the messages of the World Congress of Families. The expansion of this campaigning platform, described by human rights lawyer Naureen Shameem as one modeled on sites like MoveOn. org, Change.org, and Avaaz.org, has greatly alarmed human rights groups worldwide. By appropriating the language of human rights to validate patriarchal, discriminatory and culturally relativist norms, Shameem explains, "the focus of what these organizations do is power oriented. A manipulation of religious arguments to increase power and undermine the universality of rights" (cited in Whyte, 2017). An undercover investigation, conducted by Open Democracy (Ramsay and Provost, 2019), unmasked CitizenGo's coordination with far-right parties in Italy and across Europe, threatening the integrity of European elections by exporting the controversial US Super PAC model of political campaigning. This model presupposes the spending of unlimited sums of money raised by corporations, associations, unions and individuals to advocate for or against political candidates. As Mary Fitzgerald and Claire Provost (2019) report, the investigative work has shed light on the existence of a "powerful, well-funded global alliance of ultra-conservatives and far right political actors, many of whom unite around an economically libertarian but socially conservative worldview." These findings may potentially explain how conservative right-wing populist movements have rapidly gained consensus and electoral support in Europe in the years of rising anti-gender mobilizations. Between 2008 and 2017, the US Christian right has spent at least US\$50 million of "dark money" to fund campaigns and advocacy in Europe (Provost and Ramsay, 2019). The power of this network of influence is most visible through the number of groups connected to the World Congress of Families, including CitizenGo, which are operating transnationally both online and offline, coordinating with far-right movements and fundraising their political races.

Conclusion

We cannot fully understand social movements without understanding the dynamic relationship and interaction with their counterparts, and how movements influence countermovements and vice versa. This chapter first introduced the anti-gender countermovement in Europe, highlighting main types of anti-gender mobilizations that have spread throughout the continent and the common logic employed by actors as a backlash and to restrain LGBTQI equality. It then presented the countermovement's intersection with specific religious and political projects, in particular the struggle of the Vatican and conservative religious groups to define and legitimize the discourse on gender in line with the Catholic doctrine, one that has become instrumental in the political mobilization of contemporary anti-gender movements and their discriminatory discourses. Finally, the chapter provided an extensive analysis of the Italian anti-gender movement, its national and transnational networks of influence, as well as the tactics and strategies employed by actors to articulate their collective interests, claims and targets.

The evidence that has been presented, in addition to a closer look at the work of the World Congress of Families (WCF), shows that traditionalist anti-gender actors have a loud collective voice. They organize across lines of nationality, religion, and discourses, through joint advocacy strategies expressed both offline and online. Working together transnationally and in a coordinated manner, these actors hold great power in both the economic and political arenas, forging communities that are constantly undermining human rights, specifically those of LGBTQI people. Nevertheless, the anti-gender countermovement has at the same time contributed to raising the public profile and salience of human rights and key issues that are relevant to LGBTQI people. It has generated an increased media interest in issues such as same-sex marriage equality, civil unions, rainbow families, among others, gaining the attention of policy-makers both nationally and transnationally, ultimately influencing policy. It has also pushed LGBTQI activists to identify a common enemy, come together and build alliances and networks with other movements beyond their community, strengthening their legitimacy and recognition. If in this chapter anti-gender actors have been put at the center of the inquiry, Chapter 3 will shift attention toward key Italian LGBTQI actors and how, through their organizational communication practices, they are mobilizing, building community and identity, and strengthening their visibility and activism.

Note

1 The "Theory of Gender" is never clearly defined. As such, it creates the impression of a conspiracy theory that can represent everything and anything from marriage equality and sexual education to reproductive and adoption rights and abortion. It is framed as a new threat to the "traditional family" and binary gender roles (Kuhar and Zobec, 2017, p. 23).

References

Amnesty International (2018) *Body Politics: A Primer on Criminalization of Sexuality and Reproduction*, London: Amnesty International Ltd.

Bianchi, L. (2017) *La Gente. Viaggio nell'Italia del risentimento*, Rome: Edizioni minimum fax.

Bracke, S., and Paternotte, D. (2016) Habemus gender: The Catholic Church and "gender ideology", *Religion & Gender*, 6 (2). doi:10.18352/rg.10167.

Buss, D.E. (1988) Robes, relics and rights: The Vatican and the Beijing Conference on women, *Social & Legal Studies*, 7 (3), 339–363. doi:10.1177/096466399800700302.

Buss, D.E. (2004) Finding the homosexual in women's studies, *International Feminist Journal of Politics*, 6 (2), 257–284.

Case, M.A. (2011) After gender the destruction of man: The Vatican's nightmare vision of the gender agenda for law, *Pace Law Review*, 31 (3), 802–817.

Case, M.A. (2016) The role of the popes in the invention of complementarity and the Vatican's anathematization of gender, *Religion & Gender*, 6 (2), 155–172.

CitizenGo (2020) What is CitizenGo? Available at: https://www.citizengo.org/en-au/about-us.

Corredor, E.S. (2019) Unpacking "gender ideology" and the global right's antigender countermovement, *Journal of Women in Culture and Society*, 44 (3).

De Guerre, Y. (2015–2016) Playing the gender card, blog. Available at: https://playingthegendercard.wordpress.com/.

della Porta, D. (2008) Eventful protest, global conflicts, paper presented at Conference of the Nordic Sociological Association, European University Institute. Available at: https://www.bc.edu/content/dam/files/schools/cas_sites/sociology/pdf/EventfulProtest.pdf.

della Porta, D. and Diani, M. (1999) *Social Movements: An Introduction*, Oxford: Blackwell.

de Mattei, R. (2014) *Gender Diktat, Origini e conseguenze di una ideologia totalitaria*, Chieti, Italy: Solfanelli.

Dorf, M.C. and Tarrow, S. (2014) Strange bedfellows: How an anticipatory countermovement brought same-sex marriage into the public arena, *Law and Social Inquiry*, 39. Available at: https://scholarship.law.cornell.edu/facpub/1446/.

Fitzgerald, M. and Provost, C. (2019) The American dark money behind Europe's Far Right, *The New York Review of Books*. Available at: https://www.nybooks.com/daily/2019/07/10/the-american-dark-money-behind-europes-far-right/.

Garbagnoli, S. (2017). Italy as a lighthouse: Anti-gender protests between the "anthropological question" and national identity, in R. Kuhar and D. Paternotte (Eds.), *Anti-Gender Campaigns in Europe: Mobilizing Against Equality*, Lanham, MD: Rowman and Littlefield, pp. 151–174.

Garbagnoli, S. and Prearo, M. (2018) *La crociata "anti-gender". Dal Vaticano alle Manif pour Tous*, Kaplan.

Il Post (2019) Il Congresso Mondiale delle Famiglie, spiegato bene. Available at: https://www.ilpost.it/2019/03/24/il-congresso-mondiale-delle-famiglie-verona/.

John Paul II (1979–1984) *The Redemption of the Body and Sacramentality of Marriage (Theology of the Body)*, Rome: L'Osservatore Romano, Available at: https://d2y1pz2y630308.cloudfront.net/2232/documents/2016/9/theology_of_the_body.pdf.

Kellner, D. (2012) *Media Spectacle and Insurrection 2011: From the Arab Uprisings to Occupy Everywhere*, London: Bloomsbury.

Kuhar, R. and Zobec, A. (2017) The anti-gender movement in Europe and the educational process in public schools, *CEPS Journal*, 7 (2).

Lavizzari, A. (2020) *Protesting Gender: The LGBTIQ Movement and its Opponents in Italy*, New York: Routledge.

March for Life (2019) video. Available at: https://www.youtube.com/watch?v=eLCYRMSmmyc.

Meyer, D.S. (2004) Protest and political opportunities, *The Annual Review of Sociology*, 30, 125–145.

Meyer, D.S., Jenness, V. and Ingram, H. (2005) *Social Movements, Public Policy, and Democracy in America*, Minneapolis, MN: University of Minnesota Press.

Mos, M. (2020) The anticipatory politics of homophobia: Explaining constitutional bans on same-sex marriage in post-communist Europe, *East European Politics*, doi:10.1080/21599165.2020.1733983. Available at: https://www.tandfonline.com/doi/full/10.1080/21599165.2020.1733983.

Parke, C. (2017) Seventeen years of tracking the World Congress of Families, Political Research Associates. Available at: https://www.politicalresearch.org/2017/05/22/seventeen-years-of-tracking-the-world-congress-of-families#sthash.WpddJxsm.gMrZpUCU.dpbs.

Paternotte, D. and Kuhar, R. (2016) The anti-gender mobilization, a European issue: Report on the meeting II, Friedrich Ebert Stiftung. Available at: https://eige.europa.eu/resources/Report%20II%20Gender%20Ideology%20-%20A%20European%20Issue.pdf.

Paternotte, D. and Kuhar, R. (2018) Disentangling and locating the "Global Right": Anti-gender campaigns in Europe, *Politics and Governance: The Feminist Project under Threat in Europe*, 6 (3), 6–19.

Pontifical Council for the Family (2003) *Lexicon: Ambiguous and Debatable Terms Regarding Family Life and Ethical Question.* Available at: www.lex icon:%20Ambiguous%20and%20Debatable%20Terms%20Regarding% 20Family%20Life%20and%20Ethical%20Question.

Pontifical Council for Justice and Peace (2004) *Compendium of the Social Doctrine of the Church*, Rome: Libreria Editrice Vaticana. Available at: http://www.vatican.va/roman_curia/pontifical_councils/justpeace/documents/ rc_pc_justpeace_doc_20060526_compendio-dott-soc_en.html.

Prearo, M. (2020) Post-osservazioni dal WCF – MALORA. Available at: https://www.researchgate.net/publication/340297226_Post-osservazioni_da l_WCF_-_MALORA.

Provost, C. andRamsay, A. (2019) Revealed: The Trump-linked US Christian 'fundamentalists' pour millions of 'dark money' into Europe, boosting the far Right, Open Democracy. Available at: https://www.opendemocracy.net/ en/5050/revealed-trump-linked-us-christian-fundamentalists-pour-million s-of-dark-money-into-europe-boosting-the-far-right/

Ramsay, A. and Provost, C. (2019) Revealed: The Trump-linked 'Super PAC' working behind the scenes to drive Europe's voters to the far right, Open Democracy. Available at: https://www.opendemocracy.net/en/5050/revealed- the-trump-linked-super-pac-working-behind-the-scenes-to-drive-europes-vo ters-to-the-far-right/.

Roma Today (2018) "L'aborto è la prima causa di femminicidio", manifesti choc per Roma: "Il Comune intervenga." Available at: https://www.roma today.it/attualita/manifesti-anti-aborto-roma-14-maggio-2018.html.

Tarrow, S. (2011) *Power in Movement*, 3rd edn, New York: Cambridge University Press.

Tilly, C. (2004) *Social Movements, 1768–2004*, Boulder, CO: Paradigm Publishers.

Treccani Instituto (2012) "Family Day," in *Treccani Enciclopedia Lessico del XXI Secolo* Available at: http://www.treccani.it/enciclopedia/family-day_% 28Lessico-del-XXI-Secolo%29/.

Vox Observatory on Human Rights (2016) The maps of intolerance. Available at: http://www.voxdiritti.it/.

Vox Observatory on Human Rights (2019) The maps of intolerance. Available at: http://www.voxdiritti.it/la-nuova-mappa-dellintolleranza-5/.

Whyte, L. (2017) They are coming for your children – the rise of CitizenGo, Open Democracy. Available at: https://www.opendemocracy.net/en/5050/ the-rise-of-citizengo/.

Zenit.org (2012) March for Life in Rome: Washington D.C. serves as model for upcoming Pro-Life march in Italy. Available at: https://zenit.org/articles/ma rch-for-life-in-rome/.

3 Subversive media activism and the rise of the movement

Media, movements and theoretical perspectives

Media is the plural for medium of communication. While different people define media differently, this book takes a broad approach that includes anything through which information and meanings are created and shared, or reality is represented and reproduced (Share and Thoman, 2007). This includes television, radio, films, books, newspapers, songs, digital art, webcomics, videos, photographs, contents on social media, and also flyers, leaflets, street art, zines, among other modes of communication. Consequently, *digital media activism* is defined as the ensemble of media and communication practices, strategies and tactics used by individuals and activists to advance various causes and claims; create and share their own media artifacts of political engagement (Clark, 2016); raise their visibility and broaden participatory action across platforms; strengthen community building and networks; and confront and resist the dominant culture using digital networked technologies, including social media.

Social movement theory and digital media activism are important foundations for the theoretical frameworks that have been developed in this book. Over the past 20 years, digital and social media have rapidly evolved, shaping history and changing people's lives and the ways in which we interact and communicate with the world and each other. We have come a long way since Facebook's birth in 2004, YouTube's first viral hits in 2005, and revolutionary news coverage on Twitter in 2006. As della Porta and Pavan (2018) argue, new forms of digital activism have "prompted a highly interdisciplinary reflection on how increased communication possibilities intertwine with the organizational and the symbolic dimensions of social movements, but also on media practices as forms of resistance in their own rights" (p. 85). Sasha Costanza-

DOI: 10.4324/9781003289951-3

Chock's (2014) concept of transmedia organizing has also informed this work, particularly for its intersections with transmedia storytelling, as elaborated by media studies scholars, and concepts borrowed from social movement studies. *Transmedia organizing* is defined as "the strategic practice of cross-platform, participatory media-making for social movement ends" (ibid., p. 131). It integrates media, communications and cultural work into movement building.

In the past two decades, the literature on social movements and digital media has rapidly increased, with scholars exploring connective and collective action using digital technologies (Bennett and Segerberg, 2012; Bimber, Flanagin, and Stohl, 2012), media culture, networks and social movements in the Internet age (Castells, 2012; Costanza-Chock, 2012), or focusing on the analysis of specific empirical cases such as the Arab Spring (Eltantawy and Wiest, 2011), the #HeForShe movement (Omoera, 2016), #BlackLivesMatter (Cox, 2017; Hillstrom, 2018a), the #MeToo movement (Hillstrom, 2018b), to name just a few. Some scholars have also studied the nature of intersectional social media activism, and its relationship to race and gender identity, for example, in the case of the Black feminist hashtag #SayHerName, created to prove that police brutality is not a single-gender issue, rather one that affects women as much as men. In this context, the hashtag spoke directly not only to women of color, but also to LGBT-identifying Black women and White-identifying users (Brown, Ray, Summers and Fraistat, 2017). The political science field and social movement studies, however, have almost entirely neglected the role of media and communications in the construction of protest movements, their collective identities, sustainability and contentious politics (della Porta and Pavan, 2018, p. 95). Moreover, limited research currently exists on the ways in which non-governmental organizations (NGOs), volunteering associations, civil society organizations (CSOs), among others, are using digital and social media as part of their organizational communication strategies (Murthy, 2018), at the same time shaping social movements, advocacy, resource mobilization, and queer activists' connections nationally and transnationally.

While activists are increasingly taking advantage of digital media activism in their social movement mobilizations, the origins of social movements as we know them today, emerged during the eighteenth century, with the rise of capitalist societies, nation-states and modern mass media systems. In Europe and America, increased literacy rates and wider access to printed books, popular newspapers, cartoons, songs and pamphlets were a critical determinant of the rise of popular politics and social movements:

Print was not just a one-way-top-down commodity, but was actually a form of association and a new kind of public forum ... that made it possible for people in widely scattered towns and regions to know of one another's actions and join across wide social and geographic divides in national social movements.

(Tarrow, 2011, pp. 60–63)

The first movements were not formally organized, rather, it was their informal social networks and person-to-person associations that brought them into existence. It was due to the advent of commercial newspapers that movements expanded transnationally:

Through print, people as far apart as Messina and Warsaw, St. Petersburg and Beijing could imagine themselves not only as Italians, Poles, Russians, and Chinese, but as Jacobins and sansculottes, radicals, and communists, and their local enemies as feudatories and rentiers, aristocrats and capitalists. The weak ties among readers of the same newspapers, members of the same reading clubs, and people who occasionally met in the marketplace became the bases for social movement mobilization.

(ibid., p. 69)

Historically, print and association greatly contributed to the development of social movements, shaping collective action and solidarity, performances and repertoires, and defining common targets for contention on local, national and global scales. Radio and later television were also powerful media in the construction of contention. The use of visual images, particularly those used to report the social movements of the 1960s and 1970s, revolutionized movement tactics by exposing injustices and revealing them to the public, contrasting movements' peaceful goals with violent police behavior and raising awareness about movements among activists within the movement, and those watching remotely. Moreover, some may argue, the Internet and digital media have also created a more pluralistic arena for political communications, easing processes of "disintermediation", ones in which "movements present themselves directly to the general public with low costs, especially facilitating resource-poor actors" (della Porta and Mosca, 2005, p. 166).

In comparison to the movements of the 1960s, 1970s, 1980s and 1990s, digital media have enabled social movements to exist as renewed networks, decentralized and non-hierarchical, more pluralistic and collaborative (Atkinson, 2010; Best, 2005; Castells, 2012; Huesca,

2001; Pickard, 2006; Stengrim, 2005). Cyberfeminists and queer scholars have also recognized the potential of peripheral digital media technologies and information networks to allow more fluid sexual minority representations (Sender, 2001), enabling constant self-invention (Turkle, 2005), and the freedom to try on genders and sexualities in online spaces (Brophy, 2010). If in the past, regulated mainstream political communication was the prerogative of middle-class conservatives, mostly using heteronormative and homophobic frames, the digital media of the twenty-first century have become mobilizing tools for the expression of voice, identity and empowerment in unprecedented creative and innovative ways.

Invisibility in early media representations

The striving for public visibility has always been at the center of Western lesbian, gay, bisexual, trans, queer and intersex (LGBTQI) advocacy efforts and struggles even before the emergence of the 1970s Gay and Lesbian Liberation Movement. While visibility and representation come with power, invisibility, in many cases, has signified powerlessness for LGBTQI people. As Vito Russo, activist, journalist and author of the book *The Celluloid Closet* (1981) explains:

> The big lie about lesbians and gay men is that we do not exist ... As expressed on screen, America was a dream which had no room for the existence of homosexuals. And, when the fact of our existence became unavoidable, we were reflected on screen and off, as dirty secrets. We have cooperated for a very long time in the maintenance of our own invisibility. And now the part is over.
>
> (cited in Sullivan, 2003)

The phenomenon of symbolic annihilation (Gross, 2003), which implies the historical non-representation or underrepresentation of specific groups by the media, has been a constant in LGBTQI history and in some countries, it is still the case. While it is beyond the scope of this book to thoroughly investigate the role of media in the politics of sexuality, in other words, the use that sexuality is put to in our culture (Probyn, 1997), it is important to acknowledge that, through various practices of signification and forms of socialization and conditioning, media and popular culture have significantly shaped the ways in which homosexuality, LGBTQI identities and gender are understood or misunderstood by mass audiences.

Ann Stoler (1995) notes that, "in identifying marginal members of the body politics, [discourses on sexuality] have mapped the moral parameters of European nations" (p. 7) and marked out those whose human rights claims were worthy of recognition and those who were not. Mary Douglas (1969) further suggests that "the very contours of the body are established through marking that seek to establish specific codes of cultural coherence." In re-inscribing the boundaries of the body along new cultural lines, homosexuality has historically been repudiated and excluded by culturally heteronormative and hegemonic identities for the purposes of social regulation and control. Much of this exclusion has occurred within and through media and the discourses of popular culture (Raymond, 2003), which played a pivotal role in normalizing compulsory heterosexuality in the name of cultural coherence, and making invisible alternative forms of sexuality that fell outside the dominant discourse.

The cultural organization of sexuality in popular discourse is most evident in Hart's (2000) study on the stages of representation of gay men on American television. Gay men first underwent a non-recognition stage in which homosexuals were heavily stereotyped and portrayed as being promiscuous, degenerate, repulsive, and incapable of having lasting relationships, as opposed to heterosexual marriage. Next, they experienced a ridicule stage where characters embodied caricature roles, for example, gay men as effeminate and lesbians as unattractive and man-haters. This stage lasted until the impact of the Gay and Lesbian Liberation Movement, where increased visibility of gay men in various social positions nationwide led to a certain level of tolerance. In the 1970s, during the regulation stage, positive gay male characters started being introduced more frequently on television, paving the way for positive representations in the 1970s and 1980s (excluding setbacks in the mid- to late-1980s, when HIV/AIDS emerged).

Different countries gradually have undergone these similar stages, at different moments in history. In Italy, while we are still far from having attained fully positive representations of both women and LGBTQI people in media and popular culture, the increasing visibility of the latter, particularly on transnational on-demand streaming platforms such as Netflix, has indeed had direct and indirect positive effects on culture and society, including: greater availability of role models for younger generations, increased awareness raising on homotransphobia, hate speech and hate crimes, growing recognition of LGBTQI rights as human rights, and increased access to knowledge and information, among others. In the following section, the historical roots of LGBTQI mobilizations and the role media have played overtly and covertly in its formation are presented.

First European mobilizations of LGBTQI social movements

The historical roots of the LGBTQI movement can be traced to Germany, to a period spanning from the 1890s and pre-World War II, as an era of tolerance and emancipation for LGBT people. The first homosexual periodical in the world, *Der Eigene* [The Unique] started publishing in Berlin from 1896 until 1932. By the 1920s, Paragraph 175 of the German Penal Code, which criminalized homosexual acts, was being applied less frequently. One year later, Dr. Magnus Hirschfeld founded the Scientific-Humanitarian Committee, the first organization promoting "justice through science" (Broich, 2017) and advocating for equal rights and non-discrimination against homosexuals. In 1921, the Institute for Sex Research in Berlin was created, followed, two years later, by the World League for Sexual Reform on a Scientific Basis. In addition to the scientific developments ongoing in Germany, Berlin was renowned worldwide as a pioneer place for bringing homosexuality into the open, with hundreds of gay cafés, bars, clubs, and cultural aggregation spaces, and the proliferation of press materials, periodicals, pamphlets, magazines and books covering LGBT and political issues (Dynes, Johansson, Percy, and Donaldson, 1990). The rise of Nazism and its ideologies on eugenics, race and gender, not only repressed the flourishing of the early LGBT movement, but also completely annihilated its existence from the public sphere by destroying every trace of its expression. Literary and artistic works, publications, and scientific records were burnt, and an estimated 10–15,000 homosexuals were deported to concentration camps. The consequences of Nazi homophobia and brutality continued in the post-war period, with survivors struggling to exist and become visible in the same society that had at once both liberated and oppressed them.

In the first years of the 1900s in England, France and other European countries, cultural circles of artists, painters, intellectuals, and writers also contributed to raising the visibility of gender and sexuality, mainly through alternative means of communication (letters, poetry, fiction, plays, novels, comics, books, among others), preparing the grounds for future political activism. As Alexander Doty (1993) suggests, "queer positions, queer readings, and queer pleasures are part of a reception space that stands simultaneously beside and within that created by heterosexual and straight positions" (p. 15). Focusing on connotative rather than denotative meanings, while not overtly queer, these cultural artifacts opened up spaces where straight people unknowingly experienced queer moments. Queerness influenced both cultural production and reception. In Italy, the oldest LGTBQI publications are the periodical *L'Archivio delle psicopatie sessuali* [Archive of Sexual Psychopathies] dating back to 1896, and the journal *Rassegna di studi sessuali* (1921–1928), published by Aldo Mieli. Still today this journal is considered the greatest contribution to sexual liberation in Italy, with entries tackling issues including divorce, sex education for youths, and homosexuality, among others. Considered the pioneer of gay militants in Italy, Mieli was active in Dr. Magnus Hirschfeld's Scientific-Humanitarian Committee (Aldrich and Wotherspoon, 2002). Shortly after the journal was published, the "Società Italiana per lo studio delle questioni sessuali" [Italian Society for Sexuality Studies] was also established. Following the footsteps of early German LGBT mobilizations, an article published in 1922 in the *Rassegna di studi sessuali* was inciting Italian homosexuals to unite and advocate for their rights. However, this was the same year in which over 20,000 soldiers, led by Mussolini, marched into Rome, officially marking the beginning of the Fascist era. In 1928, when the publishing company was closed, Mieli, a Jewish homosexual activist, eventually fled to France to escape persecution.

American mobilizations and the modern Gay and Lesbian Liberation Movement

Social movements are born and exist at the intersection of politics, networks and media activism. And yet, the literature of both LGBT Studies and Media Studies has overlooked the importance of the earliest forms of LGBTQI grassroots media activism that have enabled oppressed people to come to voice, moving beyond the boundaries of state censorship and repression, into spaces of disruption and radical openness. As discussed above, central to LGBTQI identity politics is the politics of visibility, one that has been the common thread of early LGBT mobilizations. Doty explains:

> If mass culture remains by, for and about straight culture, it will be so through our silences, or by our continued acquiescence to such cultural paradigms as connotation, subcultures, subtexting, the closet, and other heterocentrist ploys positioning straightness as the norm.
>
> (1993, p. 104)

Therefore, looking at the grassroots media activism and cultural resistance practices that have taken place on the margins, and which have created the Gay and Lesbian Liberation Movement in the first place, is one step forward toward overturning those cultural and critical conventions that construct queerness as connotation, bringing outside of the closet the queerness in and of cultural texts, as well as in media practices.

Before the rise of the modern Gay and Lesbian Liberation Movement, spaces of resistance for grassroots media production existed in the United States, serving as the foundation for future LGBTQI rights mobilizations. In the 1900s, censorship became for the movement "a productive form of power, that was not merely privative, but formative as well" (Butler, 1997, p. 133), a site of both contestation and possibility, a space of resistance for the production of counter-hegemonic discourse, ones that have offered discursive possibilities to re-imagine new worlds, as well as new queer identities. This is evident in the archives of the GLBT Historical Society, which preserves national and international pioneering periodicals in LGBTQI history. One of the first recorded gay newsletters, "Friendship and Freedom," was produced in Chicago in 1924–1925. Banned by police and the postal authorities after just two issues, no copies are known to exist. Limited numbers of copies of overtly gay periodicals were also circulating in private circles between 1945–1948, while *The Hobby Directory* (1948) reached a wider audience due to its subtly and ambivalent coded queer contents. By the 1950s, pro-LGBT periodicals sent by U.S. mail had become key advocacy tools for reaching larger groups of people, even though censorship persisted.

The evolution of mass media in the 1960s and 1970s was certainly a turning point in LGBTQI culture and advocacy, where a variety of commercial, grassroots, and underground press publications and magazines started being created and distributed both nationally and transnationally, covering stories and topics underreported in mainstream media (even if criminal censorship laws were still in place). In the United States, while the outbreak of gay rioting at the Greenwich Village Stonewall Inn bar (27 June 1969) symbolically marks the new era of the Gay and Lesbian Liberation Movement, it was over a decade earlier (between 1958 and 1962), with three important U.S. Supreme Court cases (*One, Inc. v. Oleson, Manual Enterprises, Inc. v. Day*, and *Sunshine Book Co. v. Summerfield*), that the Warren Court's liberalization of obscenity law and protections of free press rights for homosexuals ensured, for the first time, the right of gay magazines to exist in the public sphere (Shepard, 2020, p. 599). Each case demonstrated the importance of traditional First Amendment theories and doctrines as instrumental in allowing LGBT citizens to identify with and create a subculture and social movement. The media were certainly a catalyst for social change and movement formation. The intersection of LGBT advocacy with the often contradictory and conflicting civil rights and feminist movements in the 1970s was also greatly strengthened through media, with unprecedented opportunities to re-envision collective action, political mobilization, lobbying and advocacy. For instance, frustrated with the male leadership of most gay liberation groups, lesbians started creating their own collectives, media artifacts, publishing houses, bookstores, newspapers, record labels and music festivals, calling for the recognition of lesbian rights among mainstream feminist and women's groups (Faderman, 2016).

If the 1970s were years of fervent political action and mobilization, in the 1980s, the LGBT rights movement suffered a strong setback as the AIDS epidemic killed 324,029 men and women in the United States between 1987 and 1998 (Rosenfeld, 2018). Nevertheless, with new action groups being created, mobilizations started to address the HIV/AIDS crisis, demanding better responses from the federal government and scientific communities. In a context of strong hostility, prejudice and stigma toward LGBT people, media, film, television, pop culture, information and awareness-raising campaigns became critical in bringing attention to HIV and AIDS, demystifying misinformation, reducing stigma, and shaping public perceptions. In addition to mainstream media efforts, the late 1980s and 1990s were also the years of the renaissance of queer media and artistic activism. Most notable examples of cultural resistance are the disruptive tactics of ACT UP/LA members who leveraged the power of emerging communication technologies in their advocacy efforts: writing letters to officials in power, participating in disruptive "phone zaps" and "fax zaps" (the equivalent of today's email bombing), distributing leaflets, putting stickers and wheat-pasted posters on the walls of public spaces, coordinating actions by teleconferencing, cell phones, and later on through emails and bulletin boards (Roth, 2017). While born in the United States, the intersectional ACT UP network quickly expanded to the transnational dimension with anti-AIDS groups being created in Sydney, Paris, London and Moscow.

Italian mobilizations leading to the first Pride

The first modern mobilization of Italian LGBT activists can be traced to 5 April 1972 during a convention organized by the Italian Sexology Center, where one of the key themes tackled during a panel discussion concerned "therapies to cure homosexuality". This was 18 years prior to the World Health Organization (WHO) depathologizing homosexuality, removing the latter from its list of "International Classification of Diseases" in May 1990. During the convention, militant groups such as the F.U.O.R.I. (the Italian Homosexual Revolutionary Front) and other European organizations peacefully gathered to protest and disrupt the convention (Barilli, 1999). Two other important events in the history of Italian mobilizations were the F.U.O.R.I. Sixth Congress and the organization of the first Homosexual Film Week, both organized in Turin in 1978. Cinema and the popular "cineforum" played an important role in community building and responding to individuals' increasing need to safely come closer together and recognize each other's existence.

The press was never a strong ally of the Italian LGBT movement. Furthermore, separation, internal political divergencies among organizations, limited exchanges and poor coordination among activists also contributed to hindering the formation of a national unified community. It was on 24 November 1979 that the first organized march of the LGBT movement (better known as Pisa79) took place in the city of Pisa, under the patronage of its Municipality and with permission from police forces. About 500 people joined this "unofficial" first Italian Gay Pride organized in honor of Dario Taddei, a homosexual man killed by a group of youths because of his sexual orientation (Russo, 2019). In the 1980s, several scattered cultural events and initiatives were organized to bring the LGBT community together, mainly in Rome and Milan. However, homosexuality was still invisible in Italian society and, when it gained visibility, it was often associated with stigmas related to AIDS. It was the 1990s that marked a turning point in the history of Italian LGBT mobilizations. To respond to the symbolic annihilation of LGBT people, in June 1994, the periodical *Babilonia* spearheaded an initiative featuring women and men publicly coming out (Cossolo, 2016). One month later, on 2 July 1994, more than 10,000 people marched in Rome during the first official Gay Pride, organized by the Circolo di Cultura Omossessuale Mario Mieli (Roma Pride, 2021). This event was the beginning of the long-awaited battle for the recognition and visibility of LGBT people's rights and freedoms, which culminated in the organization of the World Pride in Rome on 8 July 2000.

Global Pride 2020: re-envisioning movement dynamics during COVID-19

According to Armstrong and Crage (2006), media also serve as "technologies of memory," ensuring that, through reproduced and commemorated particular set of practices, collective memories stay alive. This was the case in the making of the "Stonewall Myth," in which institutionalized media routines and rituals played a critical role not only in propagating the survival of the myth over time and spreading it around the world, but also in creating the frames that are still being employed today in the organization of annual national and international commemorative events such as the Gay Pride Month, the International Day Against Homophobia, Transphobia and Biphobia (IDAHOT), World AIDS Day, the International Transgender Day of Visibility, the International Lesbian Day, the Intersex Awareness Day, among others.

Memories stay, technologies evolve, and their evolution has an immense potential not only to strengthen remembrance about LGBTQI history and struggles among youths, families and future generations, but also to mobilize action and create a deeper sense of empathy, solidarity and understanding toward individual subjects and diverse communities. The quintessential example of how media routines and rituals have enhanced the feeling of "being there together" lies in the world's biggest LGBTQI celebration ever organized, the #PrideWorldwide social campaign (Exist.Resist.Persist) that took place on 27 June 2020. This event also exposed the ways in which teams of volunteers from the European Pride Organisers Association, Inter-Pride, the US Association of Prides, Fierté Canada Pride, Orgullo Latin America, UK Pride Organisers Network, CSD Deutschland, Pride Netwerk Nederland, Svenska Pride, and Sydney Gay and Lesbian Mardi Gras (covering the Asia Pacific and Oceania regions), have pooled their resources together and, through coordinated organizational communication strategies, have made this global event happen, fostering a powerful sense of virtual community, mobilizing resources, raising funds and strengthening LGBTQI activists' connections nationally and transnationally.

With hundreds of marches and events cancelled or postponed due to the COVID-19 pandemic, the Global Pride 2020 reached 57 million viewers and provided the LGBTQI community the opportunity to come together and celebrate diversity and equality beyond the spatial and physical restrictions posed by COVID-19. Partnerships were established with media organizations such as Google, YouTube, Facebook, iHeart radio, Revry, and Time Out, and 24 hours of content were streamed from Pride organizations, activists, civil society groups, politicians and world leaders across a multitude of media platforms. This event marked a turning point in digital media convergence for global pride mobilizations. The strong organizational communication strategy that was put in place, and which ensured the success of the event's unfolding and visibility, is a reminder of the fundamental importance of factoring in and budgeting for media and digital communications resources and skills in contemporary (online and offline) social movements' mobilizations.

During the Global Pride 2020, a team of almost 70 volunteers communication and outreach professionals were mobilized to broadcast the event on the globalpride2020.org website, Facebook, Instagram, Twitter, TikTok, and Todrick Hall's YouTube channel. The collaboration that was established between the Communication Lead (from the European Pride Organisers Association in Denmark), a multi-country Communications Team of 17 digital and social media experts, graphic designers, public relations officers, 19 members of the Outreach Team, and 33 members of the Contents Production Team, was both ideal and one of a kind. At the same time, as will be discussed in the coming chapters, it must be said that the synergies created during this event do not reflect the daily experiences of the majority of national and local organizations and peripheral players of the LGBTQI movement in Italy and in the rest of the world, who still face numerous challenges when it comes to organizational communications, strategic planning, media and outreach capacities, funding and resource mobilization.

Experiences from the Global Pride and historical mobilizations have shown that the relationship between the LGBTQI community and the media has always been a complex and contradictory one. If, on one hand, the media hold the promise of freedom from invisibility and isolation, on the other hand, they may also endanger users by exposing them to online hate, harassment, discrimination and negative stereotyping. Barnhurst explains this paradox:

> Since the 1960s, queers have become increasingly visible in the media. Queer identities in community life and politics may rely in the twenty-first century on the prevailing media landscape. And yet visibility, like other semantic and semiotic forms, contains its own contradictions. The paradoxes of visibility are many: spurring tolerance through harmful stereotyping, diminishing isolation at the cost of activism, trading assimilation for equality, and converting radicalism into a market niche. Signaling the existence of queer persons may aim for inclusion in public discourse, but, through simultaneous contrast, the assertion contains its inevitable opposition: Queers are different and cannot go unremarked.
>
> (2007, p. 1)

To complicate further this relationship, the power asymmetries that exist within the LGBTQI movement itself cannot be ignored. As Eve Ng (2017) points out, "for LGBT advocacy via digital media, privileged segments of LGBT communities are more likely to shape the agendas," for example, Western subjects versus non-Western subjects. This is also reflected in the analysis of country representatives holding leadership and decision-making positions in the organization of the Global Pride 2020, with Team Leaders coming from the Netherlands, the USA, Switzerland and Denmark (countries ranking as the most LGBTQI-friendly). Disparities also concern the global North/Global South, freedom of expression in gay-friendly states versus oppressive states with anti-gay sentiments, unequal access to technology and the Internet, language (where contents are mainly in English), class, gender, race, ethnicity, religion, disability, among other socio-economic dimensions of inequality. In the case of the Global Pride 2020, it must be acknowledged, however, that several team members from Russia, North Macedonia, Lithuania and Italy, countries ranking at the bottom of the ILGA-Europe Rainbow Map and Index (2020), which assesses the legal and policy situation of LGBTI people in Europe, also contributed to the organization of the event. Moreover, a "Watching Safely Guide" was created on the main website (globalpride2020.org) by Hadi Damien from the Beirut Pride in Lebanon, with guidance for more marginalized and oppressed audiences on how to safely watch the global pride, engage with the event on social media, create safe user profiles, and respond to anti-LGBTQI cyber-attacks (trolls, virus, counter-hate speech strategies and reporting).

Conclusion

The relationship between the LGBTQI community and the media has always been a complex and contradictory one, as well as a greatly under-researched subject. However, as this chapter has shown, grassroots media activism and cultural resistance practices have been a constant in the history of the Gay and Lesbian Liberation Movement, both in Europe and in the United States, enabling oppressed people to come to voice, move beyond the boundaries of state censorship and repression, and create spaces of disruption and radical openness. Historically, as well as in present times, media practices and rituals have also become a catalyst for the transition from symbolic annihilation and non-recognition of LGBTQI people, to more mainstream and positive representations, contributing to community building and strengthening identity and visibility. As social movements and activists are increasingly taking advantage of the opportunities provided by the wide range of communication tools and platforms to organize their networks, form collective identities and develop new languages of resistance to counteract anti-gender and homophobic discourse, Chapter 4 will analyze key actors in the Italian LGBTQI movement and their organizational communication practices. In particular, attention is directed to how activists succeed in their transmedia organizing and their ability to reach audiences in their advocacy efforts. Their media capacity and priorities will also be explored, as well as their relationship building with media and reporters, and ability to forge partnerships with other organizations and networks that may have strengthened their media work.

References

Aldrich, R. and Wotherspoon, G. (2002) *Who's Who in Gay and Lesbian History*, London : Routledge.

Armstrong, E.A. and Crage, S.M. (2006) Movements and memory: The making of the Stonewall myth, *American Sociology Review*, doi:10.1177/000312240607100502.

Atkinson, J.D. (2010) *Alternative Media and Politics of Resistance: A Communication Perspective*, New York: Peter Lang.

Barilli, G.R. (1999) *Il Movimento Gay in Italia*, Milan: Giangiacomo Feltrinelli.

Barnhurst, K.G. (2007) *Media/Queered, Visibility and Its Discontents*, New York: Peter Lang.

Bennett, L.W. and Segerberg, A. (2012) The logic of connective action, *Information, Communication and Society*, 15 (5), 739–768.

Best, K. (2005) Rethinking the globalization movement: Toward a cultural theory of contemporary democracy and communication, *Communication and Critical/Cultural Studies*, 2, 214–237. doi:10.1080/14791420500198555.

Bimber, B.A., Flanagin, A.J., and Stohl, C. (2012) *Collective Action in Organizations: Interaction and Engagement in an Era of Technological Change*, New York: Cambridge University Press.

Broich, J. (2017) How the Nazis destroyed the first gay rights movement, *The Conversation*, Available at: https://theconversation.com/how-the-nazis-destroyed-the-first-gay-rights-movement-80354.

Brophy, J.E. (2010) Developing a corporeal cyberfeminism: Beyond cyberutopia, *New Media & Society*, 12 (6), 929–945. doi:10.1177/1461444809350901.

Brown, M., Ray, R., Summers, E. and Fraistat, N. (2017) #SayHerName: Case study of intersectional social media activism, *Ethnic and Racial Studies*, 40 (11), 1831–1846, doi:10.1080/01419870.2017.1334934.

Butler, J. (1997) *Excitable Speech: A Politics of the Performative*, London: Routledge.

Castells, M. (2012) *Networks of Outrage and Hope: Social Movements in the Internet Age*, Malden, MA: Polity Press.

Clark, L.S. (2016) Participants on the margins: #BlackLivesMatter and the role that shared artifacts of engagement played among minoritized political newcomers on Snapchat, Facebook and Twitter, *International Journal of Communication*, 10, 235–253.

Cossolo, F. (2016) *Storia del movimento LGBT Italiano: 1994*. Available at: www.Gay.it.

Costanza-Chock, S. (2012) Mic check! Media cultures and the Occupy movement, *Social Movement Studies*, 11, 375–385. doi:10.1080/14742837.2012.710746.

Costanza-Chock, S. (2014) *Out of the Shadows, Into the Streets! Transmedia Organizing and the Immigrant Rights Movement*, Cambridge, MA: The MIT Press.

Cox, J.M. (2017) The source of a movement: Making the case for social media as an informational source using Black Lives Matter, *Ethnic and Racial Studies*, 40 (11), 1847–1854. doi:10.1080/01419870.2017.1334935.

della Porta, D. and Mosca, L. (2005) Global net for global movements? A network of networks for a movement of movements, *Journal of Public Policy*, 25 (1), 165–190. doi:10.1017/S0143814X05000255.

della Porta, D. and Pavan, E. (2018) The nexus between media, communication and social movements: Looking back and the way forward, in G. Meikle (Ed.), *The Routledge Companion to Media and Activism*, New York: Routledge.

Doty, A. (1993) *Making Things Perfectly Queer: Interpreting Mass Culture*, Minneapolis, MN: University of Minnesota Press.

Douglas, M. (1969) *Purity and Danger*, London: Routledge & Kegan Paul.

Dynes, W.R., Johansson, W., Percy, W.A., and Donaldson, S. (1990). *Encyclopedia of Homosexuality*, New York: Garland Publishing Company. Eltantawy, N. and Wiest, J.B. (2011) The Arab Spring, Social media in the Egyptian revolution: reconsidering resource mobilization theory, *International Journal of Communication*, 5. Available at: https://ijoc.org/index.php/ijoc/article/view/1242/597.

Faderman, L. (2016) *The Gay Revolution: The Story of the Struggle*, New York: Simon & Schuster.

Gross, L. (2003) Out of the mainstream: Sexual minorities and the mass media, in G. Dines, and J.M. Humez (Eds.), *Gender, Race and Class in Media: A Text-Reader*, Thousand Oaks, CA: SAGE.

Hart, K.P. (2000) Representing gay men on American television, *The Journal of Men's Studies*, 9 (1), 59–79. doi:10.3149/jms.0901.59.

Hillstrom, L.C. (2018a) *Black Lives Matter: From a Moment to a Movement*, New York: ABC-CLIO.

Hillstrom, L.C. (2018b) *The #MeToo Movement*, New York: ABC-CLIO.

Huesca, R. (2001) Conceptual contributions of new social movements to development communication research, *Communication Theory*, 11 (4), 415–433, doi:10.1111/j.1468-2885.2001.tb00251.x.

ILGA-Europe (2020) Rainbow Map and Index 2020. Available at: https://www.ilga-europe.org/rainboweurope/2020.

Murthy, D. (2018) Introduction to social media, activism, and organizations, *Social Media +Society*, 4 (1). Available at: https://journals.sagepub.com/doi/full/10.1177/2056305117750716.

Ng, E. (2017) Media and LGBT advocacy: Visibility and transnationalism in a digital age, in H. Tumber and S. Waisbord (Eds.), *The Routledge Companion to Media and Human Rights*, New York: Routledge.

Omoera, O.S. (2016) Can social media set the agenda in addressing violence against women? *World Scientific News*, 60, 40–50.

Probyn, E. (1997) Michel Foucault and the uses of sexuality, in A. Medhurst and S.R. Munt (Eds.), *Lesbian and Gay Studies*, London: Cassell, pp. 133–146.

Raymond, D. (2003) Popular culture and queer representation: A critical perspective, in G. Dines and J.M. Humez (Eds.), *Gender, Race and Class in Media: A Text-Reader*, Thousand Oaks, CA: SAGE.

Roma Pride (2021) La Storia. Available at: romapride.it.

Rosenfeld, D. (2018) The AIDS epidemic's lasting impact on gay men, blog, The British Academy. Available at: https://www.thebritishacademy.ac.uk/blog/aids-epidemic-lasting-impact-gay-men/.

Roth, B. (2017) *The Life and Death of ACT UP/LA: Anti-AIDS Activism in Los Angeles from the 1980s to the 2000s*, Cambridge: Cambridge University Press, doi:10.1017/9781316226940.002.

Russo, E. (2019) Il Pride in Italia: storia di un'onda che non si è mai infranta, *Bossy, Beyond Stereotypes*. Available at: https://www.bossy.it/il-pride-in-italia-storia.html.

Sender, K. (2001) Gay readers, consumers, and a dominant gay habitus: 25 years of the Advocate magazine, *Journal of Communication*, 51 (1), 73–99.

Share, J. and Thoman, E. (2007) *Teaching Democracy: A Media Literacy Approach*, Los Angeles, CA: The National Center for Preservation of Democracy.

Shepard, J.M. (2020) The First Amendment and the roots of LGBT rights law: Censorship in the early homophile era, 1958–1962, *William and Mary Journal of Race, Gender, and Social Justice*, 26 (3). Available at: https://scholarship.law.wm.edu/cgi/viewcontent.cgi?article=1530andcontext=wmjowl.

Stengrim, L. (2005) Negotiating postmodern democracy, political activism, and knowledge production: Indymedia's grassroots and e-savvy answer to media oligopoly, *Communication and Critical/Cultural Studies*, 2 (4), 281–304.

Stoler, A.L. (1995) *Race and the Education of Desire: Foucault's History of Sexuality and the Colonial Order of Things*, Durham, NC: Duke University Press.

Sullivan, N. (2003) *A Critical Introduction to Queer Theory*, New York: New York University Press.

Tarrow, T. (2011) *Power in Movement: Social Movements and Contentious Politics*, Cambridge: Cambridge University Press.

Turkle, S. (2005) *The Second Self: Computers and the Human Spirit*, Cambridge, MA: MIT Press.

4 Organizational communication practices of Italian LGBTQI activists

Introduction

Italy is a country with a vast number of diverse LGBTQI organizations and players, that, in line with a core-periphery network structure (Borgatti and Everett, 1999), can be clustered and analyzed as three groups: core, periphery, and semi-periphery actors. *Core actors* encompass institutionalized national organizations, associations, governmental and ministerial departments involved in the promotion and protection of LGBTQI rights and non-discrimination based on sexual orientation. Entrenched in the social system, they have not only developed connections among themselves, but also established recognition, credibility and legitimacy. Compared to periphery actors, the core has greater exposure, more access to resources, and is more effective in mobilizing support (Cattani and Ferriani, 2008). *Periphery actors* are activists and individuals working on the margins, joining non-formal associations, and engaging in bottom-up cultural resistance. These actors are loosely connected to the core as well as with each other. By standing on the margins of the network, they can be exposed to different sources of inspiration, facilitating more creative outcomes, performances and counter-responses, and bringing a fresh perspective to the mainstream system (Schilling, 2005). Finally, *semi-periphery actors* are national organizations, associations, and individuals who occupy multiple positions and characteristics and who stand somewhere in-between the core and the periphery.

While Anna Lavizzari (2020) has provided a comprehensive analysis of the LGBTQI movement in Italy, using a mix of queer and social movement methodologies, her work has mainly focused on the way gender affects social movement structures and processes, and how in turn, social movements affect gender roles and identity. Gender and sexuality dynamics have been positioned at the center of her study. This

DOI: 10.4324/9781003289951-4

book aims to build on previous work, but differs from the latter in that it directs its attention to the organizational communications practices of LGBTQI actors in Italy, and their potential in strengthening networks and alliances, shaping movement mobilizations, and ultimately advancing and communicating effectively a more emancipatory agenda for gender and human rights. In the process of building actors' digital profiles and identifying their organizational communication practices, tracing their geographic scope, networks and alliances, and the discourses and positions taken in their advocacy work, a mixed methods approach was employed. A multi-site situational analysis was used to map relations between networks and organizations, and develop theoretical samples of research sites. Word clouds and mind mapping tools enabled the discovery of five overarching thematic areas that LGBTQI actors in Italy are currently working on (see Figure 4.1): multi-issues, including equality and marriage; fighting discrimination and gender-based violence; health, HIV and disability; school, sports and youths; migration; and sex workers' rights and protection (mainly core actors with greater resources); culture and education (core and semi-periphery actors); family (core and semi-periphery actors); faith and homosexuality (semi-periphery and periphery actors) and media (core and periphery). Semi-structured interviews with activists also provided more in-depth insights of major discourses, positions and practices that were not necessarily visible through the analyzed online media channels and digital artifacts.

Digital profiles of LGBTQI actors

While it would have been impossible to analyze all Italian LGBTQI organizations, several key actors working across thematic clusters have

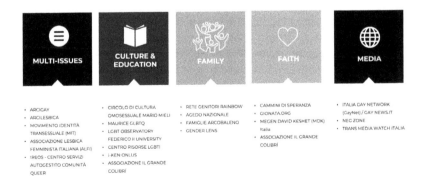

Figure 4.1 Actors' key thematic areas of work

been selected, analyzed and studied on the basis of their successful promotion and protection of LGBTQI rights, as well as their meaningful digital media practices and cultural resistance work. This chapter outlines the main actors working on multi-issues, culture and education, family, faith and homosexuality and their organizational communication practices, namely, the extent of their audience reach, media capacity and networks, and the priority impact of their communication's work.

Actors working on multi-issues

National organizations working on multiple issues have been identified mainly as core institutionalized actors. These include: Arcigay, Arcilesbica, Movimento Identità Transessuale (MIT), Associazione Lesbica Femminista Italiana (ALFI), and Ireos – Centro Servizi Autogestito Comunità Queer. Members of ILGA Europe, an advocacy group promoting the interests of lesbian, gay, bisexual, trans and intersex people in Europe and Central Asia, these organizations engage in multiple networks, strengthening ties with local, national and transnational allies during particular events, mobilizations, projects and initiatives. Key overarching thematic issues at the center of activists' work include: equality and marriage; fighting discrimination and gender-based violence; health, HIV and disability; school, sports and youths; migration; and sex workers' rights and protection.

Audience reach

While none of the interviewed actors working on multi-issues reported having an official written organizational communication and social media strategy or plan in place (with the exception of few communication officers following informal plans), each was able to identify its target audience within the LGBTQI community, mainly based on the direct beneficiaries of their services, projects and initiatives. Arcigay, ALFI and MIT stressed that while it is of utmost importance to reach out to LGBTQI community members, it is of equal importance not to leave out the general public that constitutes the Italian population, as well as European publics. This was also stressed in Ireos' statute. "An accurate, credible and responsible communication has the power to educate people, dismantle prejudice, stereotypes and ignorance and bring about social change both among the general public and within the LGBTQI community itself," affirmed Natascia Maesi (interview on 12 November 2020), who is responsible for Gender Policy and Training in Rete Donne Arcigay. At the same time, Mario di Martino, former Vice President of the MIT, warned that there is no one-size-fits-all approach to organizational communication (interview on 28 October 2020). The LGBTQI community is made up of people with different needs and struggles and these must be seriously understood and taken into account when developing communication strategies, plans and activities to prevent causing harm. For example, di Martino explained the MIT has learned that social media campaigns do not work when advocating for sex workers' rights, "Sometimes, it is the power of invisibility that protects individuals the most, especially in the workplace" (interview on 28 October 2020). This is true when considering migrant or undocumented sex workers in Italy who may face more dangers and challenges compared to documented sex workers. In this case, the use of social media applications, such as Telegram, may be more effective due to their private networking and communication functionalities.

The institutional character that enables the classification of these organizations into "core actors" must not be misled into believing the latter have in place a better-funded, more standardized, homogeneous organizational communication strategy. As a matter of fact, all actors in the network reported that communication is not only never budgeted for in their financial plans as a stand-alone activity, but is also never recognized as paid work for internal staff members or volunteers. There was a general consensus that the stigma on communication as being a "soft skill" without measurable business impact is still very prevalent in the Italian culture. This has definitely contributed to pushing organizational communications to the margins, undervaluing and underfunding it, consequently also hindering the development of much-needed capacity building programs.

With its own Press Office, Communication Group, up-to-date website infrastructure and active social media channels, Arcigay is the strongest actor in the LGBTQI community when it comes to organizational communication and digital media activism. As Italy's largest organization in terms of number of volunteers and activists, Arcigay operates on the national territory through 70 local committees and affiliated associations, reaching thousands of people with its services, initiatives and resources. Often considered the go-to organization for mainstream journalists covering LGBTQI issues of national interest, Arcigay mostly uses an institutional tone and pays close attention to how its discourses are being framed. The reality is different for ALFI, a much more recently established association, founded in 2018, and operating through its local networks in Bergamo (XX BERGAMO), Naples (Le maree), Perugia (Omaphalos), and Udine Treviso (LUNE).

Active mainly on Facebook and Instagram, and through monthly newsletters sent to members, ALFI recognizes the importance of establishing a relationship with journalists, nevertheless, currently it has reported having limited interactions with the latter, other than occasionally sharing press releases. A strong willingness to build bridges with mainstream media was expressed, particularly to increase the visibility and acceptance of lesbian, bisexual, transgender and intersex women, subjects that too often are invisible in mainstream media narratives.

Media coverage of the transgender community adds another layer of complexity to the relationship between journalists, activists and LGBTQI people. Founded in 1979 to advocate for the recognition of trans identity and respect for the dignity and rights of trans people, the MIT is considered one of the oldest associations in the country, and is currently active on the national territory through its offices in Turin, Milan, Florence, Rome, Bologna and Treviso. While visibility and awareness of the transgender community are on the rise within popular culture (also through exposure to mainstream Netflix shows such as *Pose*, or *Orange is the New Black* and *Transparent*), Italy ranks number one in Europe when it comes to homicides of trans and/or gender-diverse people. As of 2020, 42 murder cases have been recorded by the Trans Murder Monitoring (TMM) project (and many more have not been reported). Transgender people are among those most affected by symbolic annihilation and inaccurate violent reporting. Cisgenderism and transphobia justify violence, discrimination and hostility against individuals whose gender identity differs from the normative gender binary system. Storm Turchi, a non-binary transgender activist and editor at Trans Media Watch Italy, explained that the majority of murder victims are trans women who are also sex workers, of foreign origins, sometimes undocumented. In the Italian national context, the stigma of sex work and racism adds up to transphobia and tends to justify homicides, normalizing murderers and blaming victims for engaging in sex work in the first place (Guerra, 2020). This is clearly reflected in crime stories, where victims are in most cases misgendered and misidentified, exploited and sensationalized, and their murders trivialized and not considered as cases of gender-based violence.

Reaching mainstream media to improve LGBTQI coverage and advocacy

Activists in Italy acknowledged that a first step toward improving the coverage of the LGBTQI community and preventing hate speech and violent discourse would be for mainstream journalists to use accurate and respectful language and terminology. Several core actors have also been involved in the formulation of UNAR's "Guidelines for a Respectful Information of LGBT People" in 2014, which were developed as part of the National LGBT Strategy (2013–2015). While this publication mentions it had the patronage of the National Order of Journalists (the organization in charge of regulating the journalistic profession in Italy), hinting at an attempt to bring closer the world of LGBTQI activists to that of journalists, the latter has publicly distanced itself from endorsing and adopting these Guidelines (Ordine dei Giornalisti, 2013). In a recent publication on Media and LGBTQIA+ people (Celotti, 2020) published by the Order of Journalists of Lombardia, Alessandro Galimberti, President of the National Order of Journalists in Lombardia reaffirmed the lack of both a specific Italian Deontological Charter or Code of Ethics focused on gender discourse, and sensitive reporting guidelines for journalists writing crime stories featuring LGBTQIA+ people. However, on 19 November 2020, led by its Commission on Equal Opportunities, the National Order of Journalists decided to amend its *Deontological Code for the Journalistic Profession* (officially enacted on 1 January 2021) and unanimously voted to include a new article on "Respecting Gender Differences."

Article 5 bis reinforces the responsibility of journalists to avoid harmful gender stereotypes and use a respectful, correct and conscious language when reporting on cases of feminicide, violence, harassment, discrimination and crime stories involving aspects related to sexual orientation and gender identity. While the amendment of the Deontological Code is an important step forward toward improving coverage of the LGBTQI community and preventing hate speech and violent discourse, words alone will not eradicate violence, prejudice, and discrimination. Capacity building of journalists and media professionals on gender-sensitive reporting is necessary and must not occur in a silo from front-line actors operating within the LGBTQI community. Mario di Martino reinforced this point by explaining that where personal relationships between journalists and activists have been established, more attention and care have been addressed to accurate gender-sensitive reporting (interview on 28 October 2020). This was the case in several stories published by mainstream media, where the point of view and voices of trans people and MIT members were given authority and legitimacy. In the case of Arcigay, Natascia Maesi and Vincenzo Brannà (Press Officer) also emphasized the importance of establishing a two-way constant communication between activists and journalists. This exchange benefits activists, in that it allows them to better understand the needs and requirements of the media establishment, and consequently, to respond knowledgeably and in a timely manner to journalistic demands. At the same time, dialogue with activists will benefit the accountability and credibility of mainstream journalism and its responsibility toward the public and society, leaving no one behind.

A second victory for the LGBTQI community took place in November 2020, with Italy's lower house of parliament's initial approval of the Zan Bill to prevent and combat discrimination and violence on the grounds of sex, gender, sexual orientation, gender identity and disability. This bill has been debated for over 20 years and predisposes harsher penalties for hate perpetrators. Named after politician Alessandro Zan (who drafted the bill), the bill is being widely opposed by right-wing parties, the Roman Catholic Church, conservative anti-gender groups, and radical and trans-exclusionary feminists, as well as Arcilesbica, a core actor that has been highly criticized by LGBTQI groups for being transphobic and violating the Statute of the Fondazione ARCI. The majority of interviewed actors reported they were closely monitoring both media and parliamentary discourses in the time period leading to the approval of the Zan Bill in Italy's lower house of parliament. Mainstream media played a critical role in raising awareness among the general public of the passing of the bill, clarifying its contents (also through LGBTQI associations' press releases and commentaries), and extending the debate transnationally. But, it has also paved the way for Catholic and anti-gender groups to disseminate fake and alarmist news to negatively influence public opinion prior the passing of the bill, for instance, disproving official EU data on homophobic crimes in Italy (Antonacci, 2020), maintaining this bill will limit the right to freedom of expression and opinion (Moia, 2020), or more extremely declaring that the passing of the Zan Bill will forbid the New and Old Testament (De Mari, 2020). On 27 October 2021, the Zan Bill was ultimately rejected by Italy's upper house Senate, further hindering the advance of provisions against homophobia and transphobia.

Nevertheless, as happened in the case of the Cirinnà Law on civil unions of 2016, the debates and advocacy efforts that have taken place in the months leading to the rejection of the Zan Bill have greatly unified and strengthened the Italian LGBTQI movement from within, even under restrictive COVID-19 measures. While activists were unable to physically gather in the streets, thousands mobilized through the *All Out Campaign*, urging both the Parliament and the Government to pass the bill. Over 70,000 signatures were collected and presented to Parliament. Deliberately created as a "no logo" campaign to promote inclusivity among organizations, the initiative ran in conjunction with core, semi periphery and periphery actors, as well as allies and supporters of the LGBTQI community. Actors are institutionally diverse, working across sectors and themes, but joining efforts to achieve one shared, common goal. These include: Arcigay, Arci, Agedo, Ali d'aquila, Cammini di Speranza, Differenza Lesbica Roma, Diversity, EDGE, Gay Center, Giosef Italy, I sentinelli di Milano, neg.zone, Polis Aperta, Progetto Giovani Cristiani LGBT, Ra.Ne, Rete Genitori Rainbow, Rete Studenti Medi, Salento Pride, 6000 Sardine, Unione degli Atei e degli Agnostici Razionalisti (UAAR) and Unione degli Universitari (UDU).

Media capacity and networks

The media capacity of core actors working on multi-issues greatly varies across all organizations, with Arcigay being the only one with a full-time Communication Team and Press Office. In most cases, volunteers with no communications background and training, including Presidents and Executive Board members, are charged with organizational communication responsibilities, including: ensuring the appropriate visibility of their organization on multiple media channels, social media management, reaching out to the community to increase membership, creating and disseminating news, events, information and services, planning social media campaigns, raising funds, and creating safe spaces for community storytelling to take place. While most of the work is done internally, several actors also hire external communication agencies to work on specific projects and initiatives. However, in Italy, it is rare to find communication and digital marketing agencies promoting contents and strategies optimized for LGBTQI audiences. "Trans communicators should be hired for a more effective communication directed toward trans audiences," maintained the MIT (interview on 28 October 2020).

When it comes to funding, all actors in the network reported that communications is not only never budgeted for in their financial plans as a stand-alone activity, but is also never recognized as paid work for internal staff members or volunteers. A small portion of the funds raised through crowdfunding platforms, membership fees, EU and government grants and projects, 5x1000 donations, and individual donors are indirectly invested in organizational communication. Interviewed actors also acknowledged the importance of establishing partnerships across national, and, most importantly, transnational networks to strengthen their media and communication work. As one of the strongest communication core actors, Arcigay recognized its great investment in human resources when collaborations are forged with other core, semi-periphery and periphery actors. However, the costs and benefits of partnerships must also be estimated and taken into account. For the MIT, partnerships with transnational networks definitely contributed to an increased visibility of the organization's work, helped build new collaborations with allies and networks, and provided capacity building opportunities, sharing and leveraging resources and costs. Likewise, ALFI highly valued partnerships with transnational and national networks, including the Euro-centralasian Lesbian* Community (ELC), a lesbian feminist and intersectional network focusing on lesbians' needs, struggles and visibility, Arcigay Rete Donne Transfemminista, Lesbix, among others. Joint communication efforts with multiple actors in the network not only greatly help boost the visibility of the association and the mainstreaming of its published contents; they also enable the exchange of knowledge and experiences of different organizations from Italy to Europe and vice versa. "Keeping up-to-date with the rest of the world, joining mailing lists, and staying connected is very important; yet, the trend of LGBTQI networks in Italy is often to work in isolation, with limited knowledge and information sharing," explained ALFI (interview on 3 November 2020).

Priority impact of actors' communication

There was general consensus among actors that organizational communication is key to establishing authority and the legitimacy of associations and activists working for the protection and promotion of LGBTQI rights; strengthening branding, identity and recognition across local, national and transnational networks; and ensuring credibility and reliability when mobilizing resources and engaging in fundraising activities. However, without a clear written communication strategy and plan in place, difficulties emerge when trying to identify present or future priorities, and assessing actors' highest communication impact. The priority impact of organizational media and communication varies greatly across organizations, and in some cases, also within one organization itself. Arcigay reported that the work conducted by different teams on a particular project and thematic issue often also determines the communication priorities.

The MIT instead, highlighted the transformative potential of blogs and vlogs in trans communication and mobilization:

> Making vlogs and watching other people's vlogs becomes a visual as well as a narrative map for trans vloggers, enabling self-construction and self-reflection as trans … No matter what the style of

the trans vlogs is, they have artistic elements, being a site for memory preservation as well as for experiential identity communication and negotiation.

(Raun, 2014)

Communicating experience and mainstreaming accurate representations of trans people are critical for creating new social and collective imaginaries. From an organizational communication perspective, di Martino, MIT's former Vice President also explained the existing risks and challenges when communicating the organization's impact to donors:

> We must find a strategic way to communicate at best the great achievements of our work and justify where funds have been allocated; at the same time, we must ensure our communication does not negatively affect our community, particularly sex workers.
>
> (interview on 28 October 2020)

The need for capacity building support to create a well-planned communication strategy was stressed.

ALFI reported that an extremely challenging task with current resources and in-house capacity, one of its main future communication priorities would be to address the psychological and social well-being of lesbian, bisexual, transgender and intersex women. According to an EU-funded study, LGBTI people are more likely to experience health inequalities due to heteronormativity or heterosexism, minority stress, experiences of victimization and discrimination, compounded by stigma (Zeeman et al., 2019). In addition, harassment, social rejection, incommunicability barriers raised by the deeply entrenched "Don't Ask, Don't Tell" culture, and poor social support are certainly contributory factors to increased risks for negative mental health outcomes. To counteract these challenges, ALFI expressed an interest in exploring how digital media and communication can be used to increase social support, strengthen community connectedness, and nourish collective self-esteem and self-acceptance of lesbian, bisexual, transgender and intersex women. An example of this work is their first social media campaign, *Empowering Lesbian Visibility*, organized in the context of the Naples Gay Pride in 2018. By rejecting and challenging oppressive socially and culturally constructed patriarchal gender norms, this campaign exalted contentious women's empowerment in the workplace, in the family, in the community, in the context of disability and mentorship positions, reminding women of their strengths, activism, agency, courage, resilience and self-determination.

Re-thinking digital media use during COVID-19

The first Western country to be hit by COVID-19 in March 2020, Italy has faced enormous challenges and losses due to its underfunded health care system, limited number of doctors, elderly and vulnerable population, and lack of preparedness and responsive action. The pandemic has indeed impacted every aspect of life, bringing additional problems to the LGBTQI community, undocumented migrants, sex workers and the homeless. All activists reported the current situation has seen many LGBTQI people isolated and with limited access to support structures. Many have been forced to move away from their families of choice, and back into unsafe and hostile domestic spaces with the risk of facing discrimination, psychological and physical abuse. Trans activists and sex workers are also worried for their survival due to the lack of pay and non-existent government support. To respond to these challenges, Italian actors have rethought how best to support the LGBTQI community through digital media and outreach efforts.

Arcigay has greatly invested in its internal and external communication infrastructure to continue its political, cultural and social activities at a distance. The organization has created *Arcigay Onlife*, a platform hosting webinar events organized by Arcigay networks (Rete Donne Transfemminista, Rete Trans* Nazionale, Arcigay Youths, Arcigay Sport, Onda Pride) and territorial committees. Facebook Live events, online political labs, film screenings and book presentations are also being organized and delivered, featuring prominent guest speakers, policy-makers and LGBTQI activists working on disparate thematic issues. "We received an extremely positive feedback from audiences who, by joining our events and networking activities, felt less isolated during quarantine," explained Natascia Maesi (interview on 12 November 2020). Migrating activities and contents online had a multiplier effect. It has enabled national associations to better exchange and share their contents with territorial committees, and the other way round. This is a salient point in that during exchanges with representatives of Arcigay's territorial groups, there was a strong feeling about the stark communication gap that exists between Arcigay's national and territorial grassroots realities. Several youths reported not being able to identify with the national communication approach and contents (including big social media campaigns) and expressed their preference in developing more localized contents that are closer to their community's realities. Nevertheless, migrating initiatives online has provided an opportunity for scaling-up activities and nationally strengthening the voice of local networks. Paradoxically, the pandemic, the increased use of easily accessible digital media platforms, and the variety of thematic issues discussed during online webinars, have also enabled Arcigay to indirectly reach more diverse audiences. The participation of non-LGBTQI activists, representatives of feminist movements, disability rights activists, faith actors, among others has opened a window of opportunity for more intersectional interventions and cross-fertilization of discourses.

The other core actors working on multi-issues did not have the same organizational communication infrastructure to consistently carry on vast activities during the lockdown period. Nevertheless, the MIT, the Consultorio Transgenere (Torre del Lago), the Associazione Transessuale Napoli (ATN), together with several other networks including the Committee for Sex Workers' Civil Rights, have taken action both offline and online, launching a crowdfunding campaign called *COVID-19 None Alone, Support Sex Workers*, hosted on the grassroots platform "Produzioni dal Basso." The urgent need to take action in support of the most vulnerable and at-risk groups of society has notably expanded and strengthened these organizations' networks, collaborations and alliances. Services and psychological support to target groups continue to be provided through online videoconferencing platforms such as Zoom, and this is the case also for ALFI. During the first wave of the virus, the organization made several attempts to organize webinars with members of the community; however, these were not very successful. Outreach efforts migrated instead to ALFI Instagram, where interviews with representatives of national LGBTQI organizations, local committee members, as well as influencers and prominent voices of the LGBTQI movement were streamed. Through the website and social media, the organization also reached out to its audience with practical advice on how to deal with the quarantine, including providing recommendations on books, Netflix documentaries, TV shows, films, games, audiobooks and podcasts.

Actors working on culture and education

Historically, art, culture and education have always played an important role in transforming the practice of LGBTQI community development. By breaking down barriers and overcoming prejudice, promoting understanding and changing perceptions, asserting identity through self-expression, culture and education are central to the promotion of social justice and human rights. National organizations working in this domain have been identified mainly as core and semi-periphery actors and include: Centro Risorse LGBTI, Circolo di Cultural Omosessuale Mario Mieli, Maurice GLBTQ, i-Ken Onlus, and the LGBT Observatory of the Federico II University in Naples. Some are members of ILGA Europe and the Federazione ARCI, others are connected to more regional and local allies, and these organizations engage in multiple networks during particular events, mobilizations, projects and initiatives. Culture and cinema, education, communications, hate speech and hate crimes, health and well-being, migration and refugees are key overarching thematic issues at the center of these activists' work.

Audience reach

Even though all organizations reported not having any official written communication and social media strategy or plan, niche contents are being created by core and semi-periphery actors to engage specific target audiences. When it comes to organizational communication and media training, Centro Risorse LGBTI is the strongest actor in the culture and education network, also due to its practical expertise in developing capacity building programs for various stakeholders, including media professionals, educational institutions and enterprises, among others. While all organizations are visible through their websites, it is on social media, particularly on Facebook, that most communication with audiences takes place. The LGBTQI community is certainly a priority audience for all, however, as Carlo Cremona, President of i-Ken Onlus (semi-periphery actor) affirmed, "Communications must go beyond sexual orientation and gender identity. The majority must be engaged in order to create an inclusive society" (interview on 2 November 2020). The experience shared by core actor Maurice GLBTQ also shows that mainstreaming communication will not necessarily attract the wider population to one's organization work. Emanuele Busconi, Vice President of the organization, explained, "While being inclusive in our communication efforts, the cultural nature of our events and activities often creates a filter. Mostly niche audiences with specific cultural interests join our organization and attend our events" (interview on 19 November 2020). LGBTQI community members (the majority youths and middle-aged people) are joined by allies from other networks and the wider community during activities of a more political nature. A similar experience was shared by the LGBT Observatory of the Federico II University, whose main target audience includes academic researchers, gender scholars, and students from Italy and abroad. Diverse languages and discourses characterize each actor, shaping their organizational communication practices and outreach efforts, consequently also determining their niche target audiences.

Establishing relationships with mainstream media

All actors working in culture and education areas reported having limited interaction with mainstream media professionals and journalists. In the context of the *Hate Crimes No More Campaign*, led by Centro Risorse LGBTI, with support from other key actors and networks (ARCI, Arcigay, Famiglie Arcobaleno, Rete Lenford, GayNet, Rete Genitori Rainbow, Ireos Firenze, Circolo Tondelli, Rete Educare alle Differenze, CESP, Rete Educare ai diritti umani), a professional external communication agency in charge of public relations and social media management was hired to ensure the professional delivery of the campaign. Valeria Roberti, President of Centro Risorse LGBTI, explained that even though journalists do not often approach the Center, they do reach out when seeking more specific information and data relevant to the organization's research interests (interview on 9 November 2020). She further stressed the willingness and need to invest in media outreach and the importance of providing technical training to both journalists and LGBTQI organizations. As mentioned earlier in this chapter, where personal relationships between journalists and activists have been established, increased opportunities open up for LGBTQI actors to be featured in news stories. For an organization of left-wing political orientation, such as Maurice GLBTQ, the Vice President explained the difficulties of being visible in mainstream media outlets. However, the organization has been featured several times in the Communist daily, *Il Manifesto*, thanks to the active support of one of its members, who is also a journalist writing for the daily. The LGBT Observatory of the Federico II University also reported that interactions with journalists mostly occur on an annual basis, concomitant with events such as the IDAHOT, World AIDS Day, and the International Day of Commemoration in memory of the victims of the Holocaust.

Media capacity and networks

The internal media and communication capacity of both core and semi-periphery actors in the culture and education network is overall limited. As for multi-issue core actors, also in this case, members of the Executive Board, Presidents and Vice-Presidents often take on the leading role of communication and social media managers, in addition to their legal, administrative and overall coordination responsibilities. Among the actors interviewed, only the LGBT Observatory of the Federico II University has a Communication Coordinator. At times, external communication agencies are hired, based on the availability of funds, grant projects and initiatives. The work of volunteers on web development and graphic design has enabled the creation of communication infrastructures for some organizations, other times, internal staff with a background in programming and digital media have supported activities. In all cases, communications is never budgeted for nor recognized as paid work for internal staff members or volunteers.

Several actors also recognized the importance of establishing partnerships with local, regional, national and transnational networks in order to strengthen their media and communication work. For Maurice GLBTQ, partnerships with local and national actors, such as the Lesbicx, a network of feminist activists, has greatly opened the path to stronger networking, building new alliances, and bringing closer to the organization activists who were not immediately identified as a main target audience of the organization. Strengthened ties with the ARCI Foundation and online sharing of knowledge and resources, as well as social media tagging, have also contributed to increasing the visibility and legitimacy of the organization, reaching beyond one's immediate network and accessing followers' networks. While currently not directly engaged in European networks, Maurice GLBTQ is part of the "Coordinamento Torino Pride GLBT," a group of LGBTQI+ associations and allies working in the Piedmont region, committed to the promotion and protection of LGBTQI+ rights through education and awareness-raising initiatives. A member of ILGA Europe, the Coordinamento Torino Pride GLBT indirectly bridges national with transnational networks, particularly during annual celebrations such as the World Day Against Homophobia and the Transgender Day of Remembrance.

The network approach is also entrenched in the work of i-Ken Onlus, a grassroots semi-periphery actor promoting art, culture and cinema mostly at the local and regional levels, through associations including the Coordinamento Festival Cinematografici della Campania [Coordination of Film Festivals in Campania], Associazione Regionale Cori Campania [Regional Association of Chorists in Campania], and the Associazione contro le mafie [Association against the Mafia]. Past partnerships with national core actors such as the National Anti-racial

Discrimination Office (UNAR), Circolo Mario Mieli, Arcigay, and mainly local municipalities, schools, universities, Naples Archibishop's curia, and local media outlets have certainly raised the visibility and legitimacy of the organization within the community. Nevertheless, partnership building comes with challenges. i-Ken President Carlo Cremona noted:

> LGBTQI organizations, especially those in Campania, too often still work in a silo, isolated and disconnected. There is also a stark gap between the core main actors operating on the national territory and in the main Italian cities, and the grassroots organizations serving local and peripherical communities.
>
> (interview on 2 November 2020)

Separatism, internal conflicts, competition in fundraising, prejudice and misconception of one another can raise barriers within the LGBTQI community. This was echoed by Professor Fabio Corbsiero and Carmine Urciuoli, Communication Coordinator at the LGBT Observatory of the Federico II University, who explained the work of the Observatory is paradoxically acknowledged more by the Northern regions of Italy and even European University networks, rather than those in Campania (interview on 4 November 2020). The lack of connection and individualistic militancy of actors at regional and national levels are also evident from the fact that neither policy-makers nor NGOs and activists use the research and reports published by the Observatory to bring forward a more informed and knowledge-based activism. The Centro Risorse LGBTI also recognized the difficulties within the LGBTQI movement to leverage actors' strengths and competencies, and the complexities of building partnerships across national networks as opposed to transnational ones.

Priority impact of actors' communication

There are infinite ways to use culture to resist or change oppressive social structures, create new empowering languages, meanings, and visions for the future, carry forward political activity, build communities and networks, or strengthen marketing and outreach efforts. The diversity of the experiences of the culture and education actors is reflected in their identified organizational media and communication current and future priorities. For Maurice GLBT, an organization highly focused on the promotion of events (targeting the majority of youths), one of the key priorities identified is to have in place a social media strategy that will enable staff to effectively plan and manage events and, at the same time, build brand engagement, initiate interactions with activists and increase attendees' participation in the activities of the organization. Social media has been informally put at the top of this actor's agenda, with several campaigns already launched on Facebook to gain support, increase membership subscriptions and boost donations. With over 6,000 Facebook followers, there is great potential for Maurice GLBT to advance meaningful social media advocacy and reach out, inform and mobilize people on particular issues and causes. However, limited knowledge among volunteers and staff on how to professionally use social media to increase their organizational communication capacity was identified as a major obstacle and need. Moreover, the uncertainties of COVID-19 and the cancelation of all face-to-face activities and services are increasingly pushing the organization to rethink its use of digital media. The limits of going digital were also acknowledged, especially when interacting with vulnerable groups such as refugees, promoting opportunities for socialization and exchange through support groups and delivering psychological counseling.

Inspired by ILGA Europe and the work of international actors, the main priority of Centro Risorse LGBTI is to strengthen the development of digital media contents and campaigns that will better inform and educate audiences on diversity issues and the LGBTQI community. This will be done through the creation of nationally relevant narratives, discourses and graphics to be mainstreamed during celebrations and commemorations of annual LGBTQI international days. As Valeria Roberti, President of the Center, explained: "Even during the celebration of such events dedicated to the diversity of our community, there are still those who get left out" (interview on 9 November 2020). For instance, non-binary or gender queer identities, intersex and asexual people are often not part of the conversation, experiencing marginalization and invisibility from the same community they identify with. If this neglect is still strong in more "LGBTQI progressive countries," then one can imagine the challenges intersex people are facing when living in conservative socio-cultural realities, such as the Italian one, where no adequate national legislation and policy exist for the protection of intersex people's rights. In this context, awareness-raising and educating the public through digital storytelling can be very powerful. But stronger collaborations and knowledge sharing between actors and networks should be established, for instance, with the Organization Intersex International Italia, the first organization in Italy fully operated by intersex people and the

Radical Association Certi Diritti, which is also working on related issues.

From an academic perspective, the LGBT Observatory of the Federico II University stressed the importance of conducting gender and sexuality research in order to fully capture the experiences and needs of LGBTQI people living in Italy and understand what is working and what is not. Professor Fabio Corbisiero made it clear: "If we wish to support the LGBT community in the best way possible, we must generate solid scientific research that will enrich the public dialogue, inform policy-makers, and strengthen the activism of LGBTQI organizations" (interview on 2 November 2020). This is currently being done with internal resources provided by the University since no financial support is currently being mobilized by institutional funders, philanthropists or European research funding organizations. Among key priorities identified by the Observatory is the need to strengthen its communication platforms in order for national and transnational audiences to easily access research, knowledge and information and establish collaborations with the National Order of Journalists to ensure a more responsible and data-driven journalistic communication on LGBTQI thematic issues. Furthermore, there was a consensus that training academics and social scientists on how to communicate gender and sexuality to the general public in a simple and clear manner, through the acquisition of practical media and communication skills, would greatly bridge research and practice and increase the understanding of LGBTQI thematic issues among the population.

As the founder and organizer of the Omovies International Homosexual, Transgender and Questioning Film Festival (the first LGBTQI-themed festival organized in Southern Italy in 2007), for i-Ken Onlus, cinematography has a political and cultural emancipatory intent, articulating activist and queer identity politics and promoting critical thinking among both film makers and audiences. Key priorities of this organization are to convey positive, progressive and inclusive representations of LGBTQI people and counteract stereotypical narratives through cinema, theater, art, music and cultural debate. Beyond the established film festival, and as an additional channel to carry forward its key priorities, i-Ken Onlus launched on 26 November 2020 its independent web LGBTChannel.tv. With invited guests from the political arena, including Vladimir Luxuria, Europe's first openly transgender parliamentarian, Deputy and activist Alessandro Zan and Loredana Raia, Vice-President of the Campania Regional Council (who launched the web TV with a dedicated intervention on preventing and counteracting discrimination and violence on the basis of sex, gender, sexual orientation, gender identity and disability), human rights activists, educators, comedians, the corAcor Napoli Rainbow Choir, musicians and volunteers are actively engaged in the creation of contents live-streamed from a confiscated property formerly owned by the Mafia. Media convergence and the use of social media to live-stream and share web TV contents as well as Omovies Film Festival news, interviews and film-makers' interventions have, on one hand, greatly strengthened the visibility of i-Ken's work; on the other, it has also brought viewers closer together during the COVID-19 lockdown period, channeling online dialogues on a variety of thematic issues.

Actors working on family

International human rights instruments recognize the family as the fundamental unit of society and there is wide consensus among United Nations monitoring bodies[1] on the existence of different forms of family. The Working Group on the Issue of Discrimination against Women in Law and in Practice clearly states that:

> The family exists in various forms. The expression "diverse famil-ies" encompasses, for example, single-parent families; families headed by women; intergenerational families including, among others, grandparents; families headed by children, such as orphans or street children; families comprising lesbian, gay, bisexual, transgender and intersex (LGBTI) persons; extended families; self-created and self-defined families; families without children; famil-ies of divorced persons; polygamous families; and non-traditional families resulting from interreligious, intercommunity or inter-caste marriages.
>
> (International Commission of Jurists, 2015, B.1. 23)

In international law and human rights treaties, the protection of the family is linked to the principle of equality and non-discrimination. While a number of states have already recognized family diversity in their national legislation, many non-traditional families are still not recognized in the majority of states. LGBT families exist throughout the world, although they are arguably more visible in Northern European and Western countries, with existing legal frameworks of rights and obligations that formalize and protect their relationships. In the context of Italy, by not being able to match the heteronormative "nat-ural family" ideal, many LGBT families still face stigma, discrimination, exclusion and marginalization, often at the hands of people and movements who claim to defend "family values." While a gain for many, the Cirinnà Law on civil unions is in fact still problematic when it comes to the legal and social recognition and protection of rainbow families. The law excludes parents with no biological ties to their children from having any parenting rights; it also does not grant the right to adopt the children of one's partner to lesbian and gay partners (step-child adoption) who are legally recognized under this law. During the months leading up to the approval of the Cirinnà Law, LGBT family actors were at the forefront of social mobilizations, participating in public debates and demanding the legal recognition of their marriage, families and children. These were the activists, the parents, the partners who had to respond to the deceptive pro-family rhetoric promoted by anti-gender movement protestors advocating for anti-LGBTQ legislation, "normalized sexuality," and the dismantling of all "nontraditional families."

In Italy, where traditional family values are still deeply rooted in the social and cultural fabric of the country, the struggle for recognition continues and it is being brought forward by national core, semi-periphery and periphery actors, including: Agedo Nazionale (association of parents, relatives and friends of LGBT+ people), Rete Genitori Rainbow (gay, lesbian, bisexual and transgender parents with children from heterosexual relationships), Famiglie Arcobaleno (Rainbow Families), and Gender Lens, a grassroots group of parents providing support to families and schools with accurate information and knowledge sharing on "gender-variant" children and adolescents. Some are members of ILGA Europe and the European Network of Parents of LGBTI+ Persons, others are connected to more regional and local allies, and these organizations and groups engage in multiple networks during particular events, mobilizations, projects and initiatives. Overarching thematic issues at the center of activists' work include: the protection and promotion of families' rights and the mutual recognition of parenthood and same-gender partnership, awareness-raising and educational initiatives to combat prejudices, discrimination and homophobia, and support services provided to families and youths.

Audience reach

The actors working in the family network greatly distinguish themselves from those described earlier in this chapter. Mainly powered by parents who have lived and experienced first-hand the inequalities and challenges affecting their families, children, and friends, these organizations carry forward their work through a sort of "parent activism" targeted to improve their children's and families' future. In Italy, the history of LGBTQI parents and their contribution as activists in the movement have been widely overlooked. In addition, it was not until 2016, when Centro Risorse LGBTI in partnership with Famiglie Arcobaleno (Rainbow Families) and Rete Genitori Rainbow launched the first survey to quantify the number of LGBTQI families on the national territory, that official data was collected. The importance of this ILGA-Europe-funded initiative was that it could render Italian LGBTQI families more visible, tell their stories and strengthen their advocacy efforts.

All organizations stressed the voluntary nature of their work, the absence of an official written communication and social media strategy or plan, and the generational digital divide when it comes to media activism and advocacy. LGBTQI families, parents who did not perform their coming out in their family of origin and with their children, as well as families who are unable to handle and understand their children's coming out, are among the main audiences targeted by these actors. The critical importance of addressing the wider public was also highly stressed. As Fiorenzo Gimelli, President of Agedo Nazionale, one of the oldest organizations established in 1993 to support families with LGBTQI children, explained, support and acceptance have a transformative impact on the health and well-being of LGBT children.

> However, the coming-out process concerns both the child and the parents. When parents share their stories through their own coming out in support of their LGBT children, this has a major impact also on society as a whole, dismantling harmful misconceptions about sexual orientation and homosexuality.
>
> (interview on 10 November 2020)

Acceptance must start within the family, but then it must also be shared and infused outside the home. This is particularly relevant in the context of Italy, where a strongly closeted culture is still the norm in many families, who are afraid of rejection, discrimination, and negative judgment from others.

Communications is extremely important for actors in the family network. When it comes to their organizational communication practices, all organizations are visible through their websites (with both Agedo Nazionale and Rete Genitori Rainbow launching their new platforms in 2020) and engaging with target audiences on social media, mainly through Facebook. The trend on social media is to share news, events and articles of interest and add comments and posts that reflect actors' stance and position toward particular issues. The importance of creating safe spaces and online forums, where rainbow parents and their partners can share their experiences with others (even by keeping their anonymity), was emphasized by Rete Genitori Rainbow. The common denominator for all these actors is the use of a respectful, empathic, and a family-friendly tone in their communications. Ivana Palieri, Co-President of Rete Genitori Rainbow, explained: "The language often used by activists could create a backlash both to our organization's advocacy efforts, and in reaching out to our target audience, one that already faces many difficulties in sharing their personal stories" (interview on 11 November 2020). While it is of the utmost importance to raise the visibility of the work of family actors, careful consideration of certain matters is being taken into account, including privacy and the respect of minors' rights. All actors also reported having had interactions with mainstream media professionals and journalists, receiving invitations to join shows on national television, giving interviews, and sharing stories in magazines. However, scrutiny is exercised when adhering to media requests in order to avoid sensationalization of LGBTQI families' stories. The main goal is to use mainstream media to convey accurate representations of LGBT parents, amplify the voices of parents of LGBT children and ultimately raise awareness among audiences that LGBTQI rights are human rights.

Media capacity and networks

The internal media and communication capacity of core, semi-periphery and periphery actors in the family network is overall limited, with Rete Genitori Rainbow reporting it has parents volunteers directly working on internal and external communication and social media activities. At times, external communication agencies are hired, based on availability of funds, grant projects and initiatives, for example, for the production of several professional advocacy videos created by organizations. Nevertheless, communication is never budgeted for nor recognized as paid work for internal members or volunteers. Age, limited digital media skills, busy schedules and family commitments, and lack of funding to hire communication professionals, were reported as the main barriers to the implementation of a well-coordinated and planned organizational communication strategy. Actors also recognized the importance of establishing partnerships with local, regional, national and transnational networks in order to strengthen their visibility. In addition to being members of ILGA Europe, the ARCI Foundation, and part of UNAR's roundtable on LGBTQI rights, core and semi-periphery organizations mobilize across regional and local networks, reaching members and allies of different age groups and interests. They also follow the trail of key LGBTQI core actors with stronger communication capacities during important national events and offline and online campaigns and mobilizations.

The benefits of interacting with diverse networks and establishing cross-movement alliances were reported by all actors. For Agedo Nazionale, the European Network of Parents of LGBTI Persons (ENP), helped both build coalitions among European organizations with a similar mandate, and strengthen the legitimacy and voice of the organization in the EU political arena. The interaction with the Forum Nazionale delle Associazioni dei Genitori della Scuola (FoNAG), which was established as a space of encounter to discuss scholastic matters with the Ministry of Education, administrative bodies, and parents' associations, and of which both Agedo and Famiglie Arcobaleno are members, enabled activists to establish a good presence in school and university networks (where the majority of other actors are struggling). Moreover, dialogue with more conservative Catholic-oriented parents' associations supporting LGBT children such as the Associazione di Genitori e Amici di Persone Omossessuali (AGAPO), has also the potential to pave the way for more inclusive advocacy efforts and sharing of knowledge and good practices. The need to work together toward a common and shared goal and leveraging each other's skills and competencies was expressed by all the family actors. The LGBTQI movement must become more intersectional when advancing their causes, for example, organizations working on children's rights and those promoting LGBTI equality will have greater legitimacy and resonance when explaining how equal marriage or civil union partnerships would respect children's rights and reduce social exclusions. The future strategy is to strengthen joint claims and cross-movement alliances and be able to communicate effectively through more strategic and well-planned media, advocacy and storytelling strategies.

Priority impact of actors' communication

Family equality activism has often been neglected in human rights and social justice discourse, one which has privileged the complex relationship between individuals and governments. As Coffin et al. (2017)

argue: "If we can encourage our societies to embrace diverse forms of families, we can make love, justice and fairness a reality for more of us" (p. 13). Placing family equality at the center of activists' strategies, discourses, and actions offers an opportunity to link human rights struggles that are usually brought forward separately, and advance them collectively by uniting social justice movements across gender, age, social groups and claims. All the family actors interviewed identified as their current and future priority the need to acquire knowledge and skills on how to effectively integrate the family equality angle into their campaigns, advocacy, media and litigation work. Rete Genitori Rainbow explained that in Italy the struggles of rainbow parents are not that different from those of heterosexual divorced couples when it comes to the recognition of parental legal rights over children. Campaigning about family and appealing to those shared values that are the foundation of a family – love, care, safety and a sense of belonging – is of critical importance to family actors' digital media activism and also to strengthen ties with potential allies.

Ivana Palieri, Co-President of Rete Genitori Rainbow, has been a champion of this approach and stressed the need to have training programs and information exchanges on LGBTQI thematic areas targeted directly to lawyers, judges, social workers, and psychologists, among others. "Lack of knowledge on the true experiences of LGBTQI families, stigma and discrimination often lead to biased and unjust verdicts in court rulings, with terrible consequences for children and families," she maintained (interview on 11 November 2020). Capacity-building priorities are twofold. On the one hand, an effective external communication strategy is needed to demystify misconceptions of and prejudice against non-traditional families; on the other hand, family actors must acquire the communication skills to create powerful messaging that will also appeal to those who do not usually support equality arguments. Where "rights-based messaging" (step-child adoption is our right!) is not effective and may scare people off, "value-based messaging" (the family may change, but a parent will always stay) can be an alternative successful route to gain wider support of those with shared values and lived experiences. Another priority that should concern not just family actors, but all actors in the LGBTQI movement is to engage in a more coordinated and united communication when addressing policy-makers and the general public. Italian LGBTQI activists must be ready to communicate as one, rather than have numerous disjointed and scattered groups. More precise and clear political claims and messaging must also be designed and carried forward in advocacy efforts, maintained Fiorenzo Gimelli, President of Agedo Nazionale (interview on 10 November 2020).

Actors working on faith and homosexuality

Mass media, digital media and popular culture have greatly influenced and shaped specific visions and ideals of religion in contemporary societies. While in the dominant public discourse, religion and homosexuality are often constructed as incompatible and the antithesis of each other (Derks and van den Berg, 2020), alternative media has opened up spaces for marginal and peripheral religious communities to call into question religious authority, cope with the deficiencies of offline traditional religious groups (Giorgi, 2019) and advance a more emancipatory and intersectional vision of religion and the expression of faith. If in the past decade, religiosity in digital environments has been explored by several scholars (Enstadt et al., 2015; Hutchings, 2017; Lövheim and Linderman, 2005; Sumiala-Seppänen et al., 2006), the online media and communication practices of periphery religious and faith actors, including LGBTQI Catholics, Christians, Jews and Muslims, and other minorities remain unexplored.

Organizations working on faith and homosexuality in Italy have been identified mainly as semi-periphery and periphery actors. These include: Cammini di Speranza, the online portal Gionata.org, the group Megen David Keshet (MDK) Italy, Associazione il Grande Colibrí, and over 50 local groups for Christian LGBT people and their families scattered from North to South on the national territory. Some are members of the Global Network of Rainbow Catholics and the European Forum of LGBT Christian Groups, others of the World Congress – Keshet Ga'avah, and the Italian Coalition for Civil Liberties and Rights (CILID), and these actors engage in multiple grassroots, local, national and transnational networks. Key overarching thematic issues at the center of volunteers' work include: faith and homosexuality, relationships with family, coming out, equality and non-discrimination.

Audience reach

LGBTQI actors exist on the periphery of their religious communities and use digital media, mainly their websites, Facebook pages, groups and blogs, to build networks and meet other community members, disseminate information and knowledge, reach and mobilize audiences, exchange experiences and construct their religious identities. The main target groups of these organizations are LGBTQI people advocating for freedom of religion, as well as non-discrimination; subjects whose rights, well-being, and dignity are seldom protected by laws and beliefs that justify religiously motivated discrimination. In Italy, the majority of LGBTQI religious actors exist within the network of the Roman Catholic Church. However, as Alberta Giorgi (2019) maintains, since their presence is not officially recognized by the latter, these groups self-identify as "Christian" rather than "Catholic."

Over the last few decades, because of its geographic position, Italy has also experienced a large-scale migration influx. This has contributed to an increasing proliferation of a diversity of faiths on the national territory, with 29.3 percent Christian Orthodox migrants from Romania and Ukraine and 29.2 percent Muslims from Morocco, Albania, Bangladesh, Pakistan and Senegal (Fondazione ISMU, 2020). According to Ciocca (2019), there are circa two and a half million Muslims in Italy, one million of whom are Italian citizens. Communication is extremely important for religious and faith actors. Il Grande Colibrí, an association of volunteers operating in local, national and transnational networks, is digitally active and has invested in breaking the invisibility and silence that surround LGBTQIA people of the Islamic faith in Italy and abroad, as well as counteracting and dismantling homophobic and Islamophobic prejudices. This actor has long offered political representation, assistance and guidance to LGBTQIA migrants, asylum seekers and refugees. Established in 2015 and with over 2,000 Facebook followers, the Magen David Keshet Italy, the first independent Jewish LGBT organization affiliated to the World Congress of LGBT Jews (Keshet Ga'avah), is also active on Italian territory, working on intersectional issues including LGBTQI rights, non-discrimination and antisemitism. By standing on the margins, most of these periphery actors express their cultural resistance and social activism through alternative media rather than mainstream journalism, challenging power structures and calling into question traditionalist and exclusionary religious views and beliefs.

Media capacity and networks

Semi-periphery and periphery actors' organizations differ in their media and communication capacity. Cammini di Speranza reported having a communications spokesperson in charge of more traditional media relations who is often contacted by journalists to discuss topics related to Catholicism and homosexuality. With the establishment of its new council in 2020, the organization expressed the need to decentralize its communication strategy through a more efficient use of social media, ensuring a participatory dialogue with younger audiences. Associazione Il Grande Colibrí and Gionata.org, on the other hand, stood out for their strong digital presence powered by well-organized and up-to-date information and knowledge management systems, hosting multilingual contents, articles, interviews, comics, engaging visuals and graphics, multimedia libraries and active social media networks.

The organizational communications of faith and homosexuality actors varies greatly in terms of media languages used (tone, style, visuals, grammar), especially when considering activists and individuals working on the margins, joining non-formal associations, and engaging in bottom-up cultural resistance. The many local groups of Christian LGBT people and their families, for example, might be loosely connected to the core as well as with each other. Nevertheless, the common thread that unites all these actors is the power of storytelling and communicating experience. Through diverse approaches and strategies, their main strength lies in the ability to deal, unpack and communicate the complexity of faith and religious discourses and responses to homosexuality. When the human subject is (mis)treated as "the aberrant Other," their role is to humanize the subject and subvert dominant and oppressive discourses with ones of empowerment and inclusion. Alessandra Gastaldi, Legal Representative of Cammini di Speranza, expressed the great challenges of being a faith actor:

> The first challenge is to communicate accurately about faith and homosexuality and demystify the negative assumptions and preconceptions ingrained in people's minds. Secondly, misunderstanding is rooted not only in Catholic circles, but also within the LGBT community itself. Most of the times, there is adversity and the misconception that everyone in the Catholic Church is 'bad'. We cannot assume the existence of one Catholic reality. Networks of people such as those who engage with Cammini di Speranza are carrying forward a peaceful message of inclusivity and equality rights. Our strength lies in counter-discourse and showing to the LGBT community that: We are here. We speak for ourselves. The Church is all of us.
>
> (interview on 5 November 2020)

While too often not enough recognized and valued as powerful agents of change, faith and religious actors (as well as family actors) play an extremely important role in Italian LGBTQI social movement mobilizations, particularly when it comes to responding to anti-gender actors, the majority of which belong to Catholic family associations. Moreover, while LGBT faith actors are sparsely interconnected to each other, they are not officially connected to the Catholic Church, even if this is what they seek. As Giorgi (2019) explains, "The mainstream attitude toward homosexuality in the Church continues to be silence and invisibility." This is also shared by the Islamic religion and Orthodox Judaism. Reclaiming space online and offline, moving from the periphery to the center, offers an important opportunity for the expression of voice, identity and experience.

More than partnerships, actors recognized the importance of establishing interfaith dialogues and exchanges with several networks, including the established Global Network of Rainbow Catholics – joining their non-discrimination and human rights campaigns, especially targeted at those countries that criminalize homosexuality and have oppressive anti-LGBTQI regimes and laws; the European Forum of LGBT Christian Groups – joining LGBT Christian Leadership Training programs to strengthen the capacity of LGBT Christian group leaders to advocate for human rights in hostile social and religious environments and conflict situations; the World Congress – Keshet Ga'avah (worldwide voice for LGBTQIA + Jews) and the Ner Tamid del Sud, the first and only recognized Reconstructionist synagogue in Calabria. At the grassroots level, numerous Italian and transnational support groups are operating locally and are interconnected with each other. Beyond faith and religious networks, close ties have also been established with human rights advocates and organizations. Several faith actors are working to protect LGBTI refugees, asylum-seekers, stateless and internally displaced people. Support for this work has been provided by the United Nations High Commissioner for Refugees (UNHCR), the Italian Coalition for Civil Liberties and Rights (CILID) and INTERSOS.

Collaborations between faith actors and their allies working on other key thematic issues are encouraged. Cammini di Speranza, for instance, has actively participated in the All Out Campaign, urging both the Parliament and the Government to pass the Zan Bill. During the COVID-19 lockdown, interfaith dialogues and webinars on the acceptance and valorization of the LGBTQI community in Reconstructionist Judaism, encounters on Women and Theology, and exchanges with the Waldensian Church, among others, have also contributed to strengthening interfaith networks advocating for the same rights. Digital listening brought local realities together as never before, explained Alessandra Gastaldi of Cammini di Speranza. "Audiences joined our webinars from Trieste to Palermo, including rural and small communities with conservative Churches and elderly priests. Digital media opened a pathway for marginal groups with limited access to our support groups" (interview on 5 November 2020). This was extremely important during the lockdown period.

Priority impact of actors' communication

For semi-periphery and periphery faith actors, narratives and digital storytelling serve as a primary form of activist engagement and self-representation. A priority in the communication activities of these actors is the giving of voice to LGBT people and ethnic and cultural minorities of different religious traditions or spiritual beliefs. Through the narration of individuals' walks of life and the promotion of inter-faith and intergenerational dialogues, the websites and media artifacts of Gionata.org and Associazione Il Grande Colibrí, as well as Cammini di Speranza's project Rèlígo, serve as sites for ideological struggle and resistance, spaces in which the power of testimony and auto-ethnography counteract the "institutionalized rejection of difference" (Lorde, 1980). Developing critical media literacy and digital story-telling skills to empower the LGBTQI community to become creators of their own meanings and agents of social change was identified as a key priority. On one hand, periphery grassroots activists must be able to tell their own stories effectively using alternative media and outreach strategies. They must also become aware of the existing semi-periphery and core spaces in the network where their digital storytelling productions can be disseminated and rendered visible, impacting other members of the community. On the other hand, organizations working on faith and homosexuality issues must have clear communication strategies and plans in place, leveraging multiple media channels and acquiring the skills needed to respond to mainstream media demands, non-governmental organizations, donors, among other stakeholders. Currently, official written communication and social media strategies and plans are absent, and media activism and advocacy efforts are not budgeted for.

Conclusion

This chapter has presented the organizational communication practices of LGBTQI actors in Italy and their potential in strengthening networks and alliances, shaping movement mobilizations, and advancing a more emancipatory agenda for gender and human rights. Actors are working across five overarching thematic areas: multi-issues (mainly core actors with greater resources), culture and education (core and semi-periphery actors), family (core and semi-periphery actors), and faith and homosexuality (semi-periphery and periphery actors). The value of using digital and social media in NGOs and volunteering associations' strategic communication practices has been recognized by all actors, particularly during the COVID-19 pandemic. In this challenging context, Italian activists have rethought how best to support the LGBTQI community through digital media and outreach efforts. They have invested in their internal and external communication infrastructure in order to continue their political, cultural and social activities at a distance. Migrating activities online had a multiplier effect. It opened new opportunities for scaling-up actions and strengthened nationally the voice of local networks. Paradoxically, the pandemic, the increased use of easily accessible digital media platforms, and the variety of thematic issues discussed during online webinars, have also enabled organizations to indirectly reach more diverse audiences. However, many organizations still struggle when it comes to developing and implementing effective communication strategies and plans that will enable them to reach their organizational goals. Furthermore, communications is not only never budgeted for in financial plans as a stand-alone activity, but also is never recognized as paid work for internal staff members or volunteers. In spite of the limited investment in media and communications, the general consensus was expressed that organizational communication is key to establishing authority and legitimacy of associations and activists working for the protection and promotion of LGBTQI rights, strengthening branding, identity and recognition across local, national and transnational networks, and ensuring credibility and reliability when mobilizing resources and building community.

Note

1 International Conference on Population and Development, principle 26(h); Beijing Declaration and Platform for Action, paras 29, 113–115; and Copenhagen Declaration and Programme for Action, principle 26(h).

References

Antonacci, M. (2020) L'UE smentisce la falsa emergenza nazionale omofobia in italia. Ecco I dati, *Pro Vita and Famiglia Onlus*. Available at: https://www.

provitaefamiglia.it/blog/lue-smentisce-la-falsa-emergenza-nazionale-om ofobia-in-italia-ecco-i-dati.

Borgatti, S.P. and Everett, M.G. (1999) Models of core/periphery structures, *Social Networks*, 21, 375–395.

Cattani, G. and Ferriani, S. (2008) A core/periphery perspective on individual creative performance: Social networks and cinematic achievements in the Hollywood film industry, *Organization Science*, 12 (6), 824–844.

Celotti, G. (2020) *Parole o-stili di vita: Media e persone LGBTQIA+*, Lombardy: Ordine dei Giornalisti della Lombardi.

Ciocca (2019) Mussulmani in Italia: Una presenza stabile e sempre più Italiana, *Lenius*, Available at: https://www.lenius.it/musulmani-in-italia/.

Coffin, A., Paradis, E., Bosanac, G., Healy, G., Ehrt, J., Hart, M., … Treadwell, S. (2017) Using family as a frame in social justice activism: A guide for activists and funders in Europe. Available at: www.reclaimingfamilyvalues. eu.

De Mari, S. (2020) Se passerà il Ddl sull'omofobia Vecchio e Nuovo Testamento saranno vietati, *Informazione Cattolica*.

Derks, M. and van den Berg, M. (2020), *Public Discourses about Homosexuality and Religion in Europe and Beyond*, Cham: Palgrave Macmillan.

Enstadt, D., Larsson. G., and Pace, E. (Eds.) (2015) *Annual Review of the Sociology of Religion: Religion and Internet*, Leiden: Koninklijke Brill NV.

Fondazione ISMU (2020) Immigrati e religioni in italia – Comunicato stampa 16.9.2020. Available at: https://www.ismu.org/immigrati-e-religioni-in-italia -comunicato-stampa-14-9-2020/.

Giorgi, A. (2019) Mediatized Catholicism: Minority voices and religious authority in the digital sphere, *Religions*, 10, 463. doi:10.3390/rel10080463.

Guerra, J. (2020) Siamo primi in Europa per omicidi di persone trans, ma l'Italia si rifiuta di riconoscere la sua transfobia, *The Vision*. Available at: https://thevision.com/attualita/europa-transfobia/.

Hutchings, T. (2017) Design and the digital Bible: Persuasive technology and religious reading, *Journal of Contemporary Religion*, 32, 205–219.

International Commission of Jurists (2015) Report. Working Group on the Issue of Discrimination against Women in Law and in Practice. Available at: https://www.icj.org/sogiunjurisprudence/report-of-the-working-group-on-the-issue-of-discrimination-against-women-in-law-and-in-practice-ahrc2940-2-ap ril-2015/.

Lavizzari, A. (2020) *Protesting Gender: The LGBTIQ Movement and its Opponents in Italy*, New York: Routledge.

Lorde, A. (1980) *Age, race, class and sex: women redefining difference*, paper presented at Copeland Colloquium. Available at: https://www.colorado.edu/ odece/sites/default/files/attached-files/rba09-sb4converted_8.pdf.

Lövheim, M., and Linderman, A.G. (2005) Constructing religious identity on the Internet, in M. Højsgaard and M. Warburg (Eds.), *Religion and Cyberspace*, New York: Routledge, pp. 121–137.

Moia, L. (2020) Diritto e libertà. Alessandro Zan: Omofobia, rispettiamo le idee, *Avvenire*. Available at: https://www.avvenire.it/attualita/pagine/omofobia-rispettiamo-le-idee.

Ordine dei Giornalisti (2013) Persone LGBT: Non c'è un codice deontologico dell'Ordine, Available at: http://old.odg.it/content/persone-lgbt-non-c'è-un-codice-deontologico-dell'ordine.

Raun, T. (2014) Video blogging as a vehicle of transformation: Exploring the intersection between trans identity and information technology, *International Journal of Cultural Studies*, 18 (3), doi:10.1177/1367877913513696.

Schilling, M.A. (2005) A 'small world' network model of cognitive insight, *Creativity Research Journal*, 2–3, 131–154.

Sumiala-Seppänen, J., Lundby, K., and Salokangas, R. (Eds.) (2006) *Implications of the Sacred in (Post)Modern Media*, Göteborg: Nordicom.

Zeeman, N.S., Browne, K., McGlynn, N., Mirandola, M., Gios, L., Davis, R., Amaddeo, F. (2019) Health4LGBTI Network: A review of lesbian, gay, bisexual, trans and intersex (LGBTI) health and healthcare inequalities, *European Journal of Public Health*, 29 (5), 974–980. https://doi.org/10.1093/eurpub/cky226.

5 Re-envisioning human rights through rhetorical activism

> Not only must Justice be done; it must also be seen to be done.
> – Sir Gordon Hewart, Lord Chief Justice of England (1922–1940)

Introduction

Contemporary media culture is a contested terrain across which different groups and competing political ideologies struggle for dominance, shaping public opinion, people's values, beliefs and behaviors. That the media are intimately connected with power is not news. That the media tend to reinforce structural and cultural violence by using a language of hatred when dealing with conflicts (including interpersonal ones), one that victimizes, demonizes, induces to anger and social divisions, is also an undeniable truth (Galtung and Lynch, 2010). Visualizing human rights and conflict has become central to our contemporary and collective understanding about what human rights are, how they are caused and how they can or cannot be protected. Communication scholars have thoroughly investigated the ways in which media, stories and symbols shape our understanding of the world through the representation and re-enactment of social and cultural norms. If, as Luke (1999) posits, the media texts of popular culture are the very texts that help shape people's understandings of social inequalities and equalities, then, everyday media texts are also suitable for communicating and teaching about social justice and human rights in contemporary cultural contexts.

Media also play a key role in monitoring, investigating and reporting on human rights and holding institutions accountable. As seen in the previous chapters, many more people, communities and organizations (both non-profit and commercial) are becoming increasingly aware of the power of their own voice in the media, and are at the

DOI: 10.4324/9781003289951-5

same time experimenting with new ways of self-expression and bringing forward their causes through digital media and innovative technologies.

The challenges and contradictions of communicating human rights

In the past two decades, scholars and several institutions have paid increasing attention to the theorization of human rights communications, particularly the role of journalists in exposing human rights abuses, and teaching them about their fundamental rights such as freedom of expression, press freedom, access to information and free speech. This has been the case mainly in developing countries and in those where repressive political regimes have imposed strong restrictions on the media to operate freely and report the truth. For example, the United Nations Educational, Scientific and Cultural Organization (UNESCO) has been a strong advocate of the human rights-based approach to journalism; one based on the principles of participation, accountability, non-discrimination, empowerment, and human rights standards. Numerous organizations have also produced training manuals for journalists and activists to report and communicate about human rights issues in a safe, accurate and sensitive manner. There is now a general consensus among journalists and human rights activists that "the media are more receptive to human rights issues today than at any time in the modern history of the media – even though the consensus doesn't extend to saying that the media cover the subject well" (ICHRP, 2002).

Starting from the post-World War II period and increasingly in the present day, visual representations have taken on a very important role in our knowledge, understanding and interpretation of suffering and violence, understood in many ways as "human rights" (Swimelar, 2014). To make injustice visible, renowned international and local NGOs, intergovernmental organizations and activists are re-inventing themselves, adding new strategies and more creative rhetorical tactics to their organizational communication practices and human rights reporting. Initially, radio, films, photographs, mainstream news, and later social media, blogs, videos, have certainly raised the interest of people in human rights issues. New media technologies such as Virtual Reality (VR) and 360-degree video and the immersive and interactive nature of the experiences enabled by these technologies, are also offering opportunities for audiences to relate and become part of victims' stories in unprecedented ways, engendering greater empathy for subjects and expanding viewers' sense of embodied presence when witnessing a crisis, disaster or human rights violation (Owen, 2015).

While a solid body of research exists on the relationship between media, conflict and war, the link between communication, peace, conflict resolution and reconciliation has often been neglected by both scholars and practitioners (Gilboa, 2009), both in the field of peace and conflict studies and media studies. Arguably, it is precisely from the analysis of the scholarship of human rights, peace or conflict journalism and the dominant war journalism (violence-oriented, propaganda-oriented, elite-oriented, and victory-oriented) that a clear understanding of the main paradigms that shape current human rights discourses and the construction of their visual representations may best be investigated and understood (not only in mainstream media, but also in alternative media productions that will be analyzed later in this chapter).

Opposing views on media representations of human rights

Visualizing human rights is considered an act of cultural resistance, one involving asymmetrical relations of power, through which different groups in their dominant and subordinate positions struggle to define and bring forward their political claims. As Swimelar argues, "image production and politics are mutually reinforcing in that they embody a power struggle and a determination of who represents what and how" (2014, p. 415) with important implications for foreign policy, state sovereignty, international relations, and most importantly, people's lives. The politics of visibility and the power to restrict freedom of expression and define who gets to speak and who must be silenced, whose reality is presented or ignored, which discourses should be privileged and which omitted, have enormous consequences for the promotion and protection of human rights. Russia and Lithuania, for instance, do not criminalize same-sex acts or forms of gender expression, however, contents related to LGBT rights or the so-called "homosexual propaganda" are restricted and banned to silence activists on the pretense of protecting children, public morals and traditional values (Article 19, 2013). In Uganda, the Anti-Homosexuality Act (2014) prohibits any promotion of homosexuality and LGBT rights and includes criminal sanctions and up to seven years imprisonment. As Human Rights Watch (2021) reports, there are at least 70 countries in the world with national laws forbidding same-sex conduct. Restrictions of LGBTQI rights are also restrictions on freedom of expression.

Two opposing views dominate the debate on human rights communications. If, on one hand, visualizing human rights can improve the prospects for peace, justice and democracy, on the other, it can also fuel and perpetuate hate, violence and injustice. Some scholars have argued (Hanitzsch, 2004; Wolfsfeld, 1997) that the work of media practitioners, in particular, journalists, is incompatible with human rights and justice, in that mainstream visual representations often overvalue violent and reactive responses to conflict, while legitimizing, naturalizing and perpetuating violence and injustice. Numerous ethical concerns emerge when visualizing human rights, including in virtual reality journalism: Will immersive experiences augment trauma or arouse discomfort when the viewer is confronted with someone else's suffering? Will new technologies pave the way for the further "commercialization of death" and the rising misery or dark tourism in destinations where human tragedies have occurred? Will audiences engage with narratives in purely voyeuristic and narcissistic ways? Will genocide and mass atrocities be turned into gaming experiences? Will visual representations reinforce "Otherness" and binary divisions of us versus them? Should victims' suffering be decontextualized and exploited to advocate for human rights? In representing human rights across all media channels, these and many other concerns cannot be ignored.

For others instead (Galtung, 1996; Hackett, 2010; Lynch, 2015; 2013; Schmidt, in Lynch and McGoldrick, 2006; Peleg, 2006; Shaw, 2011b) a complementary human rights and peace approach to media culture and digital storytelling is crucial to understanding justice and working toward reconciliation and peace building. Shaw (2011b) defines human rights journalism as a "diagnostic style of reporting which offers a critical reflection of the experience and needs of the victims and perpetrators of (physical, cultural and structural) human rights violations" (p. 46). One of the aims of this practice is to provide strong contextualization concerning human rights violations in order to prevent more violence from escalating. Both human rights journalism and peace journalism distance themselves from the notion of neutral and detached journalism, and stand for a more compassionate reporting, one with the moral responsibility to deeply identify and understand the root causes of conflicts and human rights violations, and find the best means of addressing them to the public.

The right to be represented

From a human rights journalism perspective, all victims of human rights violations deserve equal media attention and coverage; however, the traditional journalism paradigm and mainstream media keep ignoring some of the world's deadliest conflicts and human rights violations. The war in the Democratic Republic of Congo (DRC) that began in the 1990s and that saw the death of more than five million people is only one of the many examples. This was called "Africa's World War" (Prunier, 2008), and yet, Western media almost completely ignored it. Even though today we find an increasing number of media representations of terror, human suffering and violence disseminated by mainstream media outlets, all contents are subject to a process of framing and selection that defines whose suffering matters for Western spectators. Hawkins maintains, "Wars in Africa are of little interest to the West because they are happening to people too far away, who are too different, living in countries that are not important enough" (in Harvey, 2012). In order to be in the media's spotlight, conflicts must also be of national and political interest. Golan explains:

> If a nation is a 'core nation', a large, economically powerful nation such as the US, China, Russia, Germany, and so on, then, it's more likely to receive coverage from the international media. If you are a 'peripheral nation', a small developing country, the chances of receiving international coverage are very low, unless something extraordinary happens.
>
> (ibid.)

The report on "The world's most neglected displacement crises" published in 2019 by the Norwegian Refugee Council (NRC), reinforces what Golan and Hawkins have suggested. When brutal violent conflicts cause more than 450,000 people to be displaced, as is the case in the English-speaking parts of Cameroon, one would expect the world to know about the scale of this ongoing crisis; yet the international media has remained silent with almost no journalists reporting from affected areas. "The lack of information and international political attention has allowed the situation to deteriorate from peaceful demonstrations to atrocities currently being committed by both sides; it also has been matched by a lack of humanitarian funding," reports the Norwegian Refugee Council (2019). The Rohingya, a Muslim minority group deprived of their citizenship in Myanmar and Bangladesh, are one of the most persecuted people in the world, and yet their voices are rarely heard in either Asian and Western media. Likewise, even if the 2017 anti-LGBT purge in the Chechen Republic which saw horrific abuses, torture and killings of suspected gay and bisexual men in unlawful detention facilities has gained some initial international media attention, less has been reported on the abuses that took place in 2018, 2019 and the present day. Many humanitarian disasters that deserve the world's attention are neglected because of the lack of media attention, among other reasons. This also has an impact on responses to the protection and promotion of human rights, and conflict resolution and peace-building efforts in those countries.

Complexities in communicating human rights

While in recent years journalists have increased their coverage of human rights issues in their reports and have covered peace initiatives to a greater extent compared to the past, very few stories are angled and edited from a human rights perspective. There are several challenges that many journalists face in reporting about human rights or from a human rights lens. While Mark Dennis, a correspondent for *Newsweek* in Yugoslavia, pointed out the difficulty in translating human rights issues into an effective media language, Roy Gutman, who investigated Bosnian Serb war crimes suggests, "some war crimes are reported inadequately in part because reporters do not know them when they see them" (ICHRP, 2002). The situation may be different in repressive countries, where journalists are more affected by human rights issues. The International Council on Human Rights Policy (ICHRP) has also been concerned with assessing the capacity of media professionals to provide reliable and accurate information about human rights issues to their public.

Moreover, media editors in Western democracies often have the misconception that human rights violations usually occur abroad and, therefore, human rights are often seen as a dimension of foreign policy. At the national level, when covering stories that deal with human rights issues, for example, refugees and migration, or racial and sexual discrimination, journalists seldom mention the standards and mechanisms that are in place and to which governments must abide. This undermines their role as watchdogs and their effort to hold their governments and institutions accountable for their wrongdoings. Another major problem is the competition for space and time and the culture of breaking news. Human rights journalism requires more time and contextualization, as issues need to be carefully and accurately explained in the context of wider political and social relations, and international human rights law. In spite of these challenges, there is a growing awareness both from journalists and citizen reporters using alternative media platforms that the media cannot stay quiet and passive when faced with what is currently happening in the world. The public has today more opportunities than ever before to cross-check news and information, and is demanding not only truth and justice, but also social change.

Rhetorical activism: communicating for social change

The fact that digital media have become important tools for disen-franchised people to come to voice, advance counter-narratives, including through pop culture, and advocate for social change beyond the boundaries of mainstream corporate media is undisputable. This is particularly true in a context where traditional journalism has often failed to offer equal media attention and accurate reporting of those most vulnerable individuals who stand on the margins. Nevertheless, as all Italian LGBTQI actors recognized, access to technology alone will not be enough to promote successful activism and empowerment. Language matters and if used as a political tactic for changing public consciousness, it can suddenly become a tool for radical social change (Del Gandio, 2008). Even if seldom recognized as such, activists are full-time communicators, constantly working toward the achievement of their goals. From the in-depth interviews conducted with Italian LGBTQI key actors, there was a general understanding and consensus that communications done badly will simply lead to bad activism, limited outreach and missed opportunities; communications done strategically will lead to good activism, increased visibility and greater impact. Whether it is the planning of a political campaign, lobbying, organizing a demonstration or rally, coordinating social movement mobilizations online and offline, or creating alternative media and digital storytelling to promote events, raise awareness about issues, struggles and experiences, communication is central to activism and resistance. The limited organizational communication capacities of LGBTQI actors, paired with their strong willingness to learn and invest in capacity building, are a call to action for a more effective rhetorical communication – one that will attract rather than alienate people, create interest among the public in the issues brought forward by each organization, and ultimately mobilize support from allies.

Rhetorical tactics: more about the human than about the rights

The traditional visual cultures that have shaped activism, humanitarian aid, and advocacy by positioning human rights, suffering and vulner-ability at the center of media representations are increasingly being questioned and reconsidered in light of new digital activism practices and cultural shifts. Today, as Pruce maintains: "It is insufficient for human rights NGOs to rely on dated tropes about sadness and grief associated to stereotypical humanitarian imagery. Human rights imagery should reflect notions of strength, empowerment, and resilience" (in Monshipouri, 2016, p. 67).

Likewise, in a moment in history where hate speech and violent language are rapidly spreading through social media platforms, activists' confrontational rhetoric, one deeply embedded in "callout culture" and often described as aggressive, outrageous, loud, rebellious, radical, unapologetic, should not be reduced to negativity or militancy (Del Gandio, 2008). As reported by the majority of activists, in Italy, "business as usual" activist rhetoric risks a backlash against the LGBTQI community. Confrontational communication might fuel hate and shaming from both activists and homophobes. This is particularly true on social media platforms, spaces that have become the safe haven for hate speech, with little action taken by tech giants to monitor, filter or remove violent contents. Rather than opting for a confrontational approach, the digital media activism that is being championed by Italian LGBTQI activists is one targeted toward educating the public about the human rights issues at stake, establishing an emotional connection to the cause, encouraging people to take action and change their behavior.

Amnesty International, renowned for its confrontational "naming and shaming" tactics, has also recently questioned the efficacy of its strategy. Coombes explains:

> The big idea is to make Amnesty's communications more about the humans than the rights. What we get from neuroscience is that we're trying to trigger a pain response, which most people reject. We need a sense of urgency, but urgency doesn't come when something bad is happening, because that's all the time. Urgency is when something bad is happening and we have this great solution that's not being used. We need to show people that suffering, but what we also need to do is show the alternative behaviours.
>
> (in Gwynn, 2019)

NGOs and activists must change their human rights narratives and be able to talk about existing solutions as much as the problems, crafting stories of empowerment rather than victimizing subjects. The importance of this approach has been accepted by the majority of Italian activists who reported that LGBTQI narratives have changed over time.

If it is true that Italian mainstream media keeps contextualizing LGBTQI stories mainly within the frames of crime and violence, as data from the Media Diversity Report 2019 shows (Boni 2020), through their digital media activism, actors have adopted a "peace lens" in their communications. Instead of emphasizing the "negatives," how the country is lagging behind when it comes to the promotion and protection of LGBTQI rights, its failure to prevent and counteract homo-/transphobia and misogyny, more emancipatory stories are being told about human rights defenders, politicians who are standing up for LGBTQI people, and community members who are fully integrated and accepted in society. An example of this narrative shift is shown in *Arci Gay Youths Coming Out Campaign* (2020) circulated mainly through Facebook and YouTube and powered by the hashtag #HoQualcosaDaDirvi (I have something to tell you). Vincenzo Brannà, Arci Gay Press Officer, explained,

> While half of our communication has to do with discourses of denunciation, we have understood that community storytelling is crucial to representing the diversity of our community members and fostering a sense of belonging and solidarity. This format may not be as appealing to mainstream news media, but it is very valuable to us.
>
> (interview on 12 November 2020)

The discourse promoted in this campaign differs from traditional coming out stories in that rather than focusing on human suffering, rejection, oppression and conflict, new voices are being heard on the positive outcomes of coming out – courage, acceptance, equality, freedom. Through short campaign videos self-produced by the LGBTQI community, the audience is able to see the world from the perspective of the subjects living out that story. This human identification has the power to change people's perceptions and understanding about the coming out experience.

Another example is presented by Agedo Nazionale in two of its media productions: the documentary film *Due Volte Genitori/Two Times Parents* (2009) (https://www.youtube.com/watch?v=ogC jA7C9xKM) focusing on parents' point of view and reaction to their children's coming out; and *Vite/Lives* (2020) (https://www.agedona zionale.org/vite/) focusing on the everyday lives of LGBT people. The narrative shift is evident when conducting a comparative analysis of the two media productions. *Two Times Parents* is organized into six chapters and constructed as a deep journey that starts from the revelatory moment of one's child coming out, to parents' experience of loss, guilt, need to understand, indignation, confrontation, and ultimately acceptance, growth and rebirth. "While still empowering, the emphasis of this documentary was mainly put on parents' suffering and struggle. This frame was used in a more primordial stage of our organization's work," explained Fiorenzo Gimelli, President of Agedo Nazionale (interview on 10 November 2020). *Lives*, on the other hand, takes a completely different approach and tone. The video series is organized into three chapters: remembering the coming out with family members and friends (Chapter 1: https://www.youtube.com/wa tch?v=eJCXlx4wL8sandt=35s), a portrait of the everyday lives of two transsexual people and their reflections on the transitioning experience (Chapter 2: https://www.youtube.com/watch?v=OBaxUmW0ekIandt= 193s), exchanges among four couples on their parenthood and families (Chapter 3: https://www.youtube.com/watch?v=ESh3TykQmDYandt= 624s). Compared to the first documentary film, in *Lives*, we see a paradigm shift in digital storytelling. The narrative discourse is centered on the shared and common human experiences of LGBT people in their everyday lives, beyond one's sexual orientation and gender identity. In these media productions, activism is expressed through subjects' coming to voice. Speaking for oneself is an act of truthfulness and empowerment in a context where discrimination, homophobia and prejudice are very much based on misrepresentations and negative stereotypes written, spoken and interpreted by outsiders. The representation of positive narratives has the power to transform common feelings of alienation, discomfort and hopelessness into self-acceptance, and raise awareness of the fact that alternative realities of acceptance and love do exist and are possible. Hence, these video productions tackle at once both the right to be represented and the right to express oneself freely.

Positive self-representation in storytelling is also captured in the series *Vite Divergenti: Storie di un Altro Genere (Divergent Lives)* (https://vimeo.com/140057684), produced by Discovery Italia for Real Time, in collaboration with the Movimento Identità Transessuale (MIT). In the 14 episodes streamed both on television (3 minutes promo) and online (full version), the diversity of Italian transgender realities is narrated in first person, directly by those who embody those realities. As Porpora Marcasciano, President of MIT, explained, "This is the first time a program of this kind is being streamed. We are giving back the voice to trans people, demanding recognition and dignity, and ensuring the correct and authentic representation of our journeys" (Il Resto del Carlino Bologna, 2015). Selected in 2016 by the Diversity

Media Awards for being one of the best television programs showcasing diversity and inclusivity, the power of self-determination fully transpires in this media production. On one hand, the videos delicately tackle both the challenges of transitioning and the stigma, discrimination and systemic inequality faced by trans people in Italy. On the other hand, they transcend prejudices (first and foremost the misconception that transsexuality equals prostitution) by putting at the forefront of the counter-discourse family bonds, love, passion, self-acceptance, and success. The positive and authentic self-representations in this program are a turning point in mainstream narratives of Italian transgender people.

Rhetorical tactics: video advocacy and artistic activism

When issues are too complex to explain in words, media, art and activism play an important role in educating audiences on human rights, challenging our ways of thinking, and inspiring people to take action. On one hand, audiences and consumers like a good video for its ability to convey information that is easy to digest, entertaining and engaging. On the other, commercial and non-commercial actors are aware that this medium can give a potentially big return on investment, can strengthen brand and organizational visibility, boost engagement, encourage social shares and reach millions at a minimal cost. At times when people are increasingly seeking out connections, sharing stories with videos also offers a great potential to humanize brands, organizations and causes, tapping into emotions in creative and engaging ways. In digital media activism campaigns spearheaded by small, medium-sized and large NGOs and intergovernmental organizations, emotion and activism have become inseparable and interdependent, and the driving force of communication for social change. As Duncombe and Lambert maintain:

> Activism moves the material world, while art moves the heart, body and soul ... what determines our political engagement is less a reasoned evaluation of all possible options and arriving upon a rational decision, and more a felt response: people are moved to think and act in certain ways.
>
> (in Meikle, 2018, p. 154)

This is not to say that facts and truth are less important in our political engagement, denunciation of human rights violations and social movement mobilizations. However, if not backed up by powerful digital media activism strategies, facts and truth alone will not be as effective in changing people's thoughts, understandings and perceptions towards particular realities of injustice. In other words, as Jason Del Gandio (2008) explains, what we are currently experiencing is a communicative gap between our actions and the public's reception of those actions. If we fail to communicate the urgent need for action to the general population, we will be unable to mobilize the critical masses necessary for profound social change.

The first example that leverages the power of emotion in digital media activism is the video *Non Siamo Fantasmi (We Are Not Ghosts)* (https://www.youtube.com/watch?v=xu2Xr-HE4UA), produced in 2020 by Blackball for Famiglie Arcobaleno. In Italy, there are thousands of rainbow families composed of LGBTQI parents, couples, singles or divorcees. While same-sex parents have been successfully raising children for decades, the law is still lagging behind when it comes to the recognition of the rights of children of rainbow families and their parents. The Cirinnà Law on civil unions of 2016 excludes parents with no biological ties to their children from having any parenting rights; it also does not grant the right to adopt the children of one's partner to lesbian and gay partners (step-child adoption) who are legally recognized under this law. This one-minute video is part of a campaign in which Famiglie Arcobaleno is demanding that these rights should be upheld by Sergio Mattarella, President of the Republic of Italy and the Italian Government.

In representing a family's daily routine, the video opens with the scene of Gaia, a young girl in the bedroom packing her backpack. The mother is calling the daughter to get ready to leave their home to go to school. Walking in the house hallway, a human figure dressed as a ghost suddenly appears behind the child and hugs her before leaving. In the next scene, the ghost accompanies Gaia to skate in the park. She falls and wipes her tears on the ghost's gown. Half-way through the video, it's Christmas and Gaia brings a gift to the ghost, a red gown. Now the child is drawing her family – her mother, herself and the ghost. In the final scenes of the video, when Gaia is about to fall asleep, the ghost is sitting by her side and reading a story. The narrator's voice is heard for the first time: "Where the State sees a ghost, Gaia sees her mother. Help rainbow parents be recognized by the law in order to guarantee full rights to our children." Gaia's other mother is unveiled and recognized.

This video received more than 4,000 views on YouTube and 61,000 views on Facebook (as of November 2021), and was praised on social media for its delicate yet powerful advocacy strategy. Many of those who commented on social media also reported having taken action by signing the petition of the #NonSiamoFantasmi Campaign after watching the video. Other than being emotionally moving, the main narrative discourse of this media production brings forward an undeniable truth and fact – the restrictions upon the "ghost parent," one to whom is even denied the right to pick up her/his children from school without a special authorization, who cannot assist her/his children during health care treatments, and who, in the case of death of the legal parent, risks seeing her/his children being adopted. It wasn't rational arguments that made this campaign successful, rather, human identification, an appeal to people's emotions and a call to action to care and act in the "best interest of the child," as enshrined in Article 3, Article 9 (separation from parents), Article 10 (family reunification), Article 18 (parental responsibilities), Article 20 (deprivation of family environment and alternative care), Article 21 (adoption) of the United Nations Convention on the Rights of the Child (UNCRC).

The power of digital storytelling is also expressed in the nationally and internationally multi-award-winning short film, *Luigi and Vincenzo* (2013) (https://www.youtube.com/watch?v=bQITkw5Vbeg) by Giuseppe Bucci, produced by i-Ken Onlus Omovies Film Festival in collaboration with the municipality of Naples. Featuring renowned actors Francesco Paolantoni and Patrizio Rispo (who contributed pro-bono to this initiative), this 4.25 minutes-long film portrays the long-lasting love of two gay men and their impossibility of ever fully expressing their affection in a society where human rights are still not an option for LGBTQI people. With over 40,000 views on YouTube and widely shared across national and transnational networks, this short film was originally meant to be showcased almost a decade ago as the Napoli Gay Pride campaign advertisement. The production is still relevant and contemporary in that, while the battle for the recognition of human rights has advanced, LGBTQI people, in particular third age or senior citizens, are still mostly invisible and their stories are not being told. As Bucci explains:

The intention was to tell the story of people whose life without rights has almost reached an end. Neglecting marriage equality to LGBTQI people means destroying the lives of both homosexuals and heterosexuals. How many more cover-up heterosexual marriages will occur? How many more children of these fake marriages will come into the world? Wouldn't it be better for children to be born from gay parents who truly love one another?

(gay.it, 2015)

The theme of universal love and the generation gap that exists also within the LGBTQI community when it comes to expressing one's identity is powerfully presented in this short film.

The scene opens with the camera facing Luigi during the early morning hours. In the background, Vincenzo is a blurred figure in the kitchen preparing the coffee. He then walks towards the camera and sits next to Luigi. Before sipping his coffee, Luigi asks Vincenzo how much sugar and milk he has added to his coffee. Vincenzo responds correctly, knowing exactly his partner's taste. "Today the coffee must be perfect," speaks Luigi with a preoccupied attitude. Vincenzo comforts him by putting his arm on the shoulder. "Please no," says Luigi, for fear someone might see them even if it's sunrise and nobody is watching. The scene then moves to Naples' subway, where the camera shoots the two men on the escalator. The choice of this setting is powerful; an allegory of their closeted life moving forward monotonously and unchanged. That day is also the gay pride. A small crowd of youths is descending the escalator in the opposite direction, showcasing their pride, happiness and openness about their sexuality. The camera focuses back on Luigi and Vincenzo's faces who seem hopeful for a better future to come for the new generation. They have missed out on their life and now that they're almost at the end of it, Vincenzo takes one step closer to his partner, holds his hand in public, breaking the secrecy of their relationship. Luigi responds with a kiss and the young crowd applauds their love. The final scene unfolds at the entrance of the hospital. Even though the two men have spent a lifetime together, Luigi is impotent and left outside with his back facing the gate. He is invisible to the State and the health care system. No legal rights are granted to him; hence he can't be at his partner's side during the medical treatment. Vincenzo's daughter, on the other hand, walks her father inside.

The movie ends with the words: "Luigi and Vincenzo, a life, a love, no rights," but the portrayal of that denial is powerfully expressed throughout the film through the couple's love and emotions. The hope for a more just future transpires. This is also in a context where in the same year this film was produced, the French parliament had just approved the bill legalizing same-sex marriage and adoption. As seen earlier in this research, the transnational dimension of the French antigender countermovement and the LGBTQI social movement had an influence on Italian mobilizations. One might argue, the passing of the same-sex marriage law in France was even a catalyst to strengthen Italy's campaigns and advance claims. The unexpected success of *Luigi and Vincenzo* in France, Norway, the USA, Canada, Brazil, Israel,

India, Taiwan, among others, clearly shows the potential of transnational media activism, digital storytelling and the arts. It also shows the universality of human rights and the importance of protecting those rights cross-culturally.

Rhetorical tactics: queer, underground, alternative webcomics

Comic books, strips, graphic novels and webcomics have always been an important site for cultural production and exploration of feminist and non-binary sexualities and identities. Composed of a mix of literary styles and born from underground comix culture, punk and grrrl zines, marginalized queers, gay erotic art, and camp humor, these cultural artifacts vary in their representations, themes and tones (educative, political, angry, explicit, funny, provocative, uncensored) and are created primarily by periphery grassroots networks for queer communities (Hall, 2013). If historically queer comics have struggled for their recognition, the advent of the internet has unleashed queer writers' artistic potential, enabling them to reclaim spaces and reach transnational audiences, express their identities and activism, and build empathy and inclusion. As Sikk notes, starting in the 1990s and 2000s, the queer comics production underwent a radical change of genre and activist strategies: "Contemporary queer comics focus on the personal and emotional struggles of young people rather than radical politics or explicit sex. Politics are expressed implicitly through affective personal narratives, and less as direct political commentary on the evening news" (in Naples, 2020, p. 330). If considered as auto-ethnographic texts, these cultural artifacts can be used to closely examine queer experiences and subjectivities, and their relationship with society and justice.

Periphery culture actor Il Grande Colibrì distinguishes itself from other Italian actors by leveraging the potential of comics in its communication and advocacy work. Covering in multiple languages the legal and socio-cultural conditions of sexual and religious minorities in Africa, America, Asia, Europe and Oceania, comics are used to illustrate news, stories, interviews, and articles featured on the organization's website and cross-shared on social media. Thematic issues the organization engages in span from human rights violations to racism, homophobia, hate speech, violence within and outside the lesbian, gay, bisexual, trans, queer, intersex and asexual (LGBTQIA) community, politics, activism, migration, arts and culture. Moreover, particular attention is being addressed to breaking the invisibility and hostile silence that surrounds LGBTQIA Muslims in Italy and dismantling homophobic and Islamophobic prejudices. In partnership with associations such as Renzo and Lucio, Certi Diritti and Les Cultures, Il Grande Colibrí is also involved in the monitoring and analysis of human rights violations against LGBTQIA people and the production of dossiers to map out their real living conditions in respective countries. To promote access to information and acknowledging the impediments of language barriers, translations of reports from major human rights NGOs such as Amnesty International and Human Rights Watch are also being disseminated in local languages to LGBTQIA migrants, asylum seekers and refugee people.

Through the translation of webcomics from LGBTQIA people in Brazil, Iran, Algeria, Malaysia, Mexico, Spain, the UK, Belgium, and Canada, activism is also expressed through cultural resistance using comics and graphic novels. The informal sharing of webcomics through digital media not only opens a space for meaningful transnational connectedness among queer people of different descent; but also enables transcultural investigations of gender politics and sexual and ethnic identities, and how these coexist and interact within and with cultures and societies. A powerful example is the graphic novel *Yousef and Farhad* (2015), which illustrates to global audiences, particularly youths, the struggle of being gay and in love in Iran. Created by Out-Right Action International in partnership with Algerian-American political cartoonist, Khalil Bendbib, and the award-winning Iranian-American author, Amir Soltani, one of the main objectives of this narrative is to reach out to Iranian families struggling with their loved ones' sexual orientation and promote a culture of tolerance, mutual respect and peaceful coexistence. Disseminated in principle as a Facebook series, and later published on OutRight Action International's website, this graphic novel portrays, on one hand, the prejudice and pain of those who refuse to accept the existence of LGBTQI people in Iran (particularly out of ignorance, cultural assumptions and negative stereotyping). On the other hand, by subverting the dominant hegemonic discourse and "placing love where it belongs: at the center of conversations about what it means to be human" (Soltani, in OutRight Action International, 2015, p. 22), powerful counter-narratives of acceptance and tolerance are being crafted through the gestures of the main characters in the comics (Yousef's uncle, the Ayatollah and ultimately even his father) who resist and subvert the dominant homophobic order. While set in Iran, the story of Yousef and Farhad could easily be transplanted to any other patriarchal and homophobic society, including Italy. The challenges and rejection the two lovers face, as well as the societal pressure their families experience, bring us back to the commonalities of LGBTQI struggles and experiences, as well as the universality of love and human rights.

Rhetorical tactics: religious resistance, communicating the journeys of queer souls

The importance of storytelling in expressing voice and activism, gaining visibility, and promoting self-understanding has been a constant in the research and analysis of faith actors' organizational communication practices. As Sanders (2020) maintains,

> Our deepest sense of who we are, our connection to the communities in which our lives are deeply embedded, each of the cherished values and principles and truths that enliven our activity and animate our imaginations, our sense of place and significance in the cosmos – all of these are shaped by stories.
>
> (p. 1)

While the majority of religious narratives are still hostile and damaging to LGBTQI lives, reinforcing invisibility, marginalization, rejection, and even leading to suicide in many cases, alternative counter-narratives exist and are increasingly being shared in periphery faith networks through digital media platforms. One example that stands out as a testament of LGBTQI Christians' digital media activism is the web-reportage Rèlígo of Cammini di Speranza. Realized by documentary photographer Simone Cerio, this project is the outcome of a five-years' research journey among LGBT Christian communities in Italy who have agreed to share their stories and in-depth reflections on the theme of sexual orientation and gender identity. Narrated through a multiplicity of digital media forms, including photography, video, audio interviews, and documentation, Rèlígo's main objective is to open up a safe space where self-identification can take place and positive stories from LGBT Christians can be heard and shared. The project starts with an introduction to the complex relationship between faith and homosexuality, and the change of discourse that took place from the time when Joseph Ratzinger was still cardinal (1986), one in which homosexuality was strongly framed as immoral and a problem to heteronormativity, until July 2013, when in the context of the World Youth Day, for the first time in history, Pope Francis declared gay people should not be marginalized but integrated into society. The main official documentation of the Catholic Roman Church dealing with homosexuality and passages from the bible are also presented in this introductory section.

The journey continues with the remembrance of the first local groups of LGBT faith activists established in Italy by the end of the 1970s and the beginning of the 1980s. Their resistance to the silence and lack of recognition from the Catholic Church and their strong sense of belonging to their faith are what pushed activists to come out of the shadows and increasingly reclaim periphery spaces. In 2010, the web portal Gionata.org was a catalyst for stronger networking of Italian LGBT Christians on the national territory; later strengthened by Cammini di Speranza, the official national association, gathering local groups of LGBT Christians. Throughout the journey, the narrative is accompanied by photographs, video and audio testimonies of Italians reflecting on love, sexuality, spirituality, family and identity. LGBT Christians, Catholics and Protestants from abroad are also featured. It is important to understand that "LGBT people are not just people who must be welcomed by the Church; they are also active agents participating in the life of the Church," explains Valentina Coletta, the first transgender woman in Italy to be a local preacher for the Methodist and Waldensian Evangelical Churches (interview with Cerio, 2018). Even though the activism of faith actors is seldom recognized, including in the wider LGBTQI social movement, the etymology of the word Religion which derives from "religo," and which translates in "to bind," is a good auspice for what Italian LGBTQI actors could become – a more united and bounded movement, pooling resources and jointly mobilizing for a common cause.

Conclusion

The field of human rights rhetoric is still dominated by opposing views and debates on whether visualizing and communicating about human rights can improve the prospects of peace, justice and democracy, or legitimize, naturalize and perpetuate violence and injustice. Nevertheless, the fact that digital media have become important tools for disenfranchised people to come to voice, advance counter-narratives and advocate for social change beyond the boundaries of mainstream corporate media cannot be disputed. Communications and language matter and, if used as political tactics for changing public consciousness, these can suddenly become tools for radical social change. Whether it is the planning of a political campaign, lobbying, organizing a demonstration or rally, coordinating social movement mobilizations online and offline, or creating alternative media and digital storytelling to promote events, raise awareness about issues, struggles and experiences, communication is central to activism and resistance. As this chapter has shown, traditional visual cultures that have shaped activism are increasingly being questioned and reconsidered in the light of new digital activism practices and cultural shifts. This is particularly true in the context of Italy, where the majority of LGBT actors reported that "business as usual" activist rhetoric risks a backlash against the community, fueling hate and shaming from both activists and homophobes. Rather than opting for a confrontational approach, the digital media activism that is being championed by Italian LGBTQI activists is one targeted toward educating the public about the human rights issues at stake, establishing an emotional connection and human identification with the cause, encouraging people to take action and change their behavior. The digital media cultural resistance practices that have been presented in this chapter fully convey this approach. Instead of emphasizing the "negatives," how the country is lagging behind when it comes to the promotion and protection of LGBTQI rights, more emancipatory stories are being told about human rights defenders, community members who are fully integrated and accepted in society, the existence of alternative realities of acceptance and love, and ultimately the universality of human rights and the importance of protecting those rights cross-culturally.

References

Article 19 (2013) Traditional values? Attempts to censor sexuality. Homosexual propaganda bans, freedom of expression and equality. Available at: https://www.article19.org/data/files/medialibrary/3637/LGBT-propaganda-report-ENGLISH.pdf.

Boni, F. (2020) Diversity Media Report 2020: ecco la ricerca annuale sulla rappresentazione inclusiva nei media italiani. Available at: https://www.gay.it/diversity-media-report-2020-ricerca-annuale-rappresentazione-inclusiva-media-italiani.

Cerio, S. (2018) Rèlígo, Cammini di Speranza.

Del Gandio, J. (2008) *Rhetoric for Radicals: A Handbook for Twenty-First Century Activists*, London: New Society Publishers.

Galtung, J. (1996) *Peace by Peaceful Means: Peace and Conflict, Development and Civilization*, London: Sage.

Galtung, J. and Lynch, J. (2010) *Reporting Conflict: New Directions in Peace Journalism*, St. Lucia, Australia: University of Queensland Press.

Gay.it (2015) Luigi e Vincenzo: intervista al regista Giuseppe Bucci, *un anno dopo*. Available at: https://www.gay.it/luigi-e-vincenzo-intervista-al-regista-giuseppe-bucci-un-anno-dopo.

Gilboa, E. (2009) Media and conflict resolution: A framework for analysis, *Marquette Law Review*, 93 (1), 87–110.

Gwynn, S. (2019) Amnesty International wants to make human rights popular, *Campaign*. Available at: https://www.campaignlive.co.uk/article/amnesty-international-wants-make-human-rights-popular/1592146.

Hackett, R. (2010) Journalism for peace and justice: Towards a comparative analysis of media paradigms, *Studies in Social Justice*, 4 (2), 179–198.

Hall, J. (2013) *No Straight Lines: Four Decades of Queer Comics*, Seattle: Gary Groth and Kim Thompson Publishers.

Hanitzsch, T. (2004) The peace journalism problem: Failure of news people – or failure on analysis? In T. Hanitzsch, M. Loffelholz and R. Mustamu (Eds.), *Agents of Peace: Public Communication and Conflict Resolution in an Asian Setting*, Jakarta: Friedrich Ebert Stiftung, pp. 185–209.

Harvey, N. (2012) Why do some conflicts get more media coverage than others?, *New Internationalist*. Available at: https://newint.org/features/2012/09/01/media-war-coverage/.

Human Rights Watch (2021) The love that dare not to speak its name, *LGBT Rights*. Available at: http://internap.hrw.org/features/features/lgbt_laws/.

ICHRP (2002) *Journalism, Media and the Challenge of Human Rights Reporting*, The International Council of Human Rights Policy.

Il Resto del Carlino Bologna (2015) Trans, le loro Viete divergenti in onda su Real Time. Available at: https://www.ilrestodelcarlino.it/bologna/cronaca/trans-vite-divergenti-1.1362679.

Luke, C. (1999) Media and Cultural Studies in Australia, *Journal of Adolescent and Adult Literacy*, 42 (8), 622–626.

Lynch, J. (2013) Critical realism, peace journalism and democracy, *Ethical Space, Institute of Communication Ethics and Abramis Academic*, 11 (1/2), 29–36.

Lynch, J. (2015) Media in peace and conflict studies. In *Communication and Peace: Mapping an Emerging Field*, New York:Routledge.

Lynch, J., and McGoldrick, A. (2006) Peace journalism, in J. Galtung, and C. Webel (Eds.), *Routledge Handbook of Peace and Conflict Studies*, Abingdon: Routledge, pp. 248–264.

Meikle, G. (2018) *The Routledge Companion to Media and Activism*, New York: Routledge.

Monshipouri, M. (2016) *Information Politics, Protests, and Human Rights in the Digital Age*, Cambridge: Cambridge University Press.

Naples, N.A. (2020) *Companion to Sexuality Studies*, Oxford: Wiley.

Norwegian Refugee Council (2019) The world's most neglected displacement crises. Available at: https://www.nrc.no/shorthand/fr/the-worlds-most-neglected-displacement-crises/index.html.

OutRight Action International (2015) *Yousef and Farhad*. OutRight Action International.

Owen, T.*et al.* (2015) *Virtual Reality Journalism*, Tow Center for Digital Journalism.

Peleg, S. (2006) Peace journalism through the lens of conflict theory: Analysis and practice, *Conflict and Communication Online*, 5 (2). www.cco.regener-online.de.

Prunier, G. (2008) *Africa's World War, Congo, the Rwandan Genocide, and the Making of a Continental Catastrophe*, Oxford: Oxford University Press.

Sanders, C.J. (2020) *Christianity, LGBTQ Suicide, and the Souls of Queer Folk*, London: Lexington Books.

Shaw, I. (2011a) Human rights journalism: A critical conceptual framework of a complimentary strand of peace journalism, in I. Shaw, J. Lynch and R. Hackett (Eds.), *Expanding Peace Journalism: Comparative and Critical Approaches*, Sydney: Sydney University Press.

Shaw, I. (2011b) *Human Rights Journalism: Advances in Reporting Distant Humanitarian Interventions*, London: Palgrave Macmillan.

Swimelar, S. (2014) Making human rights visible through photography and film, in A. Mihr, and M. Gibney (Eds.), *The SAGE Handbook of Human Rights*. vol. I, Los Angeles, CA: Sage.

Wolfsfeld, G. (1997) Promoting peace through the news media: Some initial lessons from the Oslo peace process, *International Journal of Press and Politics*, 2 (4), 52–70.

6 Effects of legislation on attitudes toward LGBTQI people

> Law and justice are not always the same. When they aren't, destroying the law may be the first step toward changing it.
>
> – Gloria Steinem

Misconceptions of freedom of expression

Recent efforts to limit hate speech in Italy have focused heavily on online expression. The country's long-standing political and economic instability has also seen increasing tensions between hate speech and freedom of expression advocates, resulting in the adoption of measures that are yet to find the right balance between the protection of freedom of expression and the prohibition of incitement to hate, discrimination, hostility, and violence (Article 19, 2018). While the right to freedom of expression is fundamental and has been recognized worldwide as a prerequisite for open and democratic societies, one must also understand that the latter is not absolute. This is particularly relevant in the Italian context where haters (including politicians) continually invoke their right to freedom of expression to justify their violent and homophobic hate speech, disregarding the harm that their words may have on individuals and minorities, and going unpunished for their violations.

Freedom of expression in international human rights treaties

There are nine core international human rights treaties which set international standards for the promotion and protection of human rights worldwide. Freedom of expression is protected by four of these treaties: the International Covenant on Civil and Political Rights (ICCPR), the International Convention on the Elimination of All

DOI: 10.4324/9781003289951-6

Forms of Racial Discrimination (ICERD), the Convention on the Rights of the Child (CRC), and the International Convention on the Protection of the Rights of All Migrant Workers and Members of their Families (ICRMW). These legal instruments complement each other, are interdependent and mutually reinforcing. By ratifying treaties, States Parties subscribe to these standards and commit to implement the rights. However, it must be said that recognition of rights on paper is not the same as people's full enjoyment of human rights in practice.

Article 19 of the Universal Declaration on Human Rights (UNDHR) is the first and most widely recognized statement of the right of freedom of expression according to which: "Everyone has the right to freedom of opinion and expression; this right includes freedom to hold opinions without interference and to seek, receive and impart information and ideas through any media and regardless of frontiers" (United Nations, 1948). According to this article, the right of freedom of expression belongs to everyone without distinction of race, sex, ethnicity, language, religion, political beliefs, among others. In addition to protecting the right to express one's opinions and "seek, receive and impart" information and ideas (including expression of views and opinions that offend, shock or disturb), this article is also generally understood to protect the right to hold opinions without interference. Even though Article 19 was written in 1948, one may argue, the language that was used is more relevant today than never before. Article 19 protects people's right to express themselves through "any media," a fundamental notion in the twenty-first century, and "regardless of frontiers," intended today as both geographical, political, and virtual.

When analyzing legally binding treaties, the right of freedom of expression, as well as the rights to hold opinions and ideas, and receive information, are most extensively expressed in Article 19 of the International Covenant on Civil and Political Rights (ICCPR)[1] in a language that resonates that used in UDHR. While freedom of expression is a fundamental and inalienable human right, it is not guaranteed in absolute terms and it carries special duties and responsibilities. As opposed to the UDHR, Article 19 (3) of the ICCPR clearly requires that certain restrictions must be provided when some rights may come into conflict with the rights of others. These restrictions are also expressed in the Convention on the Rights of the Child (CRC) under Article 13 (2) and in the International Convention on the Protection of the Rights of All Migrant Workers and Members of their Families (ICMW) under Article 13.

In the Report of the Special Rapporteur on the promotion and protection of the right to freedom of opinion and expression (2011), former UN Special Rapporteur Frank La Rue clearly stated, legitimate types of information which may be restricted under Article 19 (3) include: child pornography (to protect the rights of children), hate speech (to protect the rights of affected individuals), defamation (to protect the rights and reputation of individuals), and advocacy of national, racial or religious hatred that incites discrimination, hostility and violence (to protect the rights of individuals, for example, their right to life). A state may exceptionally limit this right provided that:

- *Any restriction must be provided by law* (principles of predictability and transparency) – the law must be formulated with precision in order to enable individuals to regulate themselves accordingly. Even though broad and vague restrictions on freedom of expression are not permitted under Article 19 (3), many countries have in place vaguely worded laws (sedition laws, internal security laws, national security laws, public order laws) that are being manipulated and interpreted to restrict people's freedom of expression.
- *It must serve one of the legitimate purposes set out in Article 19, paragraph 3, namely, the respect of the rights or reputation of others, and protection of national security or public order, or of public health or morals.* This restriction cannot be used to protect the government from exposure of wrongdoing and to censor critical views of media professionals and individuals.
- *Must be necessary and the least restrictive means required to achieve the purposes listed in paragraph 3 (a) and (b) (principles of necessity and proportionality).* In this context, necessity implies that there are no other solutions to achieve the purposes listed in the article other than restricting or limiting freedom of expression. In addition, proportionality means that the least restrictive measures should be applied if these are able to achieve the same objective achievable through more restrictive measures.

Any legislation put in place to restrict freedom of expression, including limiting hate speech, must conform to the strict requirements of this three-part test. Article 20(2) of the ICCPR also provides that any advocacy of national, racial, or religious hatred that constitutes incitement to discrimination, hostility, or violence must be prohibited by law.

European instruments protecting the right to freedom of expression

At the European level, the European Convention on Human Rights and Fundamental Freedoms (ECHR) was adopted in 1950 by the

Council of Europe and entered into force in 1953. Almost all States Parties to the ECHR have integrated the Convention into their national legislation, making it binding on domestic courts and public authorities. Article 10 of the ECHR[2] guarantees the right to freedom of expression and is structured in two paragraphs, one defining the freedoms protected; the other outlining the conditions in which State Parties may legitimately restrict the right to freedom of expression. As in ICCPR, also Article 10 (2) of the ECHR sets a three-part test for the legitimate restriction of freedom of expression. Restrictions are allowed for protecting territorial integrity or public safety, for preventing the disclosure of information received in confidence, or for maintaining the authority and impartiality of the judiciary. It is also worth mentioning that in 2014, the Council of the European Union adopted the EU Human Rights Guidelines on Freedom of Expression Online and Offline as a practical guidance for the prevention of violations of freedom of expression and the promotion of this right.

Even though most states have signed international treaties and have committed to guaranteeing freedom of expression, this right has been continuously under debate worldwide with tensions between those opposing moralistic, protectionist and paternalistic justifications for limiting freedom of expression, and those who believe freedom of expression should be regulated in the interests of national security and public order, preventing hate speech, discrimination, and violence. Contemporary debates around legitimate restrictions to freedom of expression are mostly in terms of harm and offence; two notions that are subjective and may have different meanings in different cultural contexts. While many liberals do not justify the fact that freedom of expression should be limited on the grounds of offence, the latter should be limited if its deemed to be harmful to others. These debates have also permeated in discussions on the Zan Bill to prevent and combat discrimination and violence on the grounds of sex, gender, sexual orientation, gender identity and disability; one that today predisposes harsher penalties for hate perpetrators.

Law 76/2016 on Civil Unions: changed attitudes or reinforced divide?

Same-sex marriage is now legal in the majority of Western Europe, with the Netherlands 20 years ago becoming the first country in the world to recognize this civil right to LGBTQI people, and Switzerland being the latest, with the Parliament adopting on 18 December 2020 an amendment to the Swiss Civil Code that allows same-sex couples to enter into marriages. Despite major changes in laws and policies surrounding the issue of same-sex marriage and the promotion of

LGBTQI human rights globally, Italy is still lagging behind. The Italian Senate passed its Law 76/2016 on civil unions as a result of the ground-breaking judgment in the case of *Oliari and Others v. Italy* (2015), in which the European Court on Human Rights found the country to have breached the European Convention on Human Rights in connection to the right to respect private and family life of homosexual people. As a matter of fact, contrary to most European countries where similar laws have been enacted as a result of political debates at the parliamentary level, in Italy, it was the judiciary who paved the way for a law on same-sex partnerships and to encourage lesbian and gay couples to fight for their rights in courts (Winkler, 2017).

For some, the law on civil unions is considered a historic step forward and arguably also a catalyst of change in the Italian public's attitudes toward homosexuals. However, even if the latter includes several provisions from civil marriage, the ongoing tensions between lesbian and gay couples' expectations of equality and, on the other hand, the insistence of separating same-sex civil unions from civil marriage, still risks reinforcing forms of discrimination on the basis of sexual orientation and relegating homosexuals to a status of inferiority. The tensions that were reflected through more than 4,000 amendments made to the bill during its drafting period result today in several inconsistencies and flaws in the Law, both in its text and at the implementation level. First of all, Article 1 frames civil unions as an institution made available exclusively to couples of the same sex and no reference is ever made to "family" except in Article 12, which entitles registered partners to agree and determine the address of their "family life" (L. 76/2016). The Law's terminology also differs from that used in the Civil Code, for example, while marriage is "celebrated," civil unions are "constituted."[3] Among other differences, Article 1(11) does not mention fidelity as registered partners' duties, which could undermine and negatively imply that gay and lesbian couples are unable to enjoy monogamous and loyal relationships. Moreover, the termination and dissolution of a civil union are much simpler and faster compared to divorce. Lastly, one of the most salient discriminatory and contested aspects of this Law concerns the removal of the step-child adoption by same-sex couples, hindering not only the legal protection of rainbow families, but also not taking into account the best interests of the child, as stated in the Convention on the Rights of the Child (1990).

At the same time, it must be said that the Law requires the same preconditions of civil marriage, namely, the absence of a pre-existing civil union or marriage and the absence of consanguinity or affinity between the partners,[4] and can be challenged on the same grounds as marriage.[5] Partners' rights and duties to provide reciprocal material and moral support and cohabitation,[6] assets partitioning, inheritance and social security are also recognized. Moreover, Article 1(20) establishes that

> in order to ensure the effectiveness of the protection of rights and the fulfillment of registered same sex partners' obligations, any provisions referring to marriage and containing the words 'spouse', 'spouses' or equivalent terminology, wherever they occur in any law, regulation, administrative deeds and collective agreements, also apply to civil unions between persons of the same sex.

The rise in support of same-sex marriage and civil unions over the past decade has pushed researchers (Ayoub and Garretson, 2017; Flores and Barclay, 2016; Askoy et al., 2018; Redman, 2018) to investigate further whether there is a correlation between policy achievements and changes in public opinion towards sexual minorities. As Redman (2018) argues,

> If the legal recognition of same-sex couples increases favorable attitudes toward these individuals, it suggests that the societal position of gays and lesbians may increase more rapidly … and that elites can have a significant influence on societal attitudes simply by passing certain types of legislation.
>
> (p. 628)

Nevertheless, according to an international study conducted by the Pew Research Center (2020), public opinion on the acceptance of homosexuality in society remains sharply divided by country, region, economic development, religious and political attitudes. While Western Europe and the Americas are generally more accepting of homosexuality, countries in Eastern Europe, Russia, Ukraine, the Middle East and sub-Saharan Africa remain less accepting. Furthermore, in the Asia-Pacific region, people generally stand between acceptance and rejection. This sharp divide in attitudes and perceptions concerning change in societal attitudes is also felt in Europe, where data from the EU-LGBTI II Survey (2020) of the European Union Agency for Fundamental Rights (FRA) shows that in Ireland, Malta and Finland, over 70 percent of respondents perceived a decrease in intolerance and violence in the past five years. On the other hand, in Poland and France, most respondents reported that both intolerance and violence have overall increased. The Pew Research Center furthermore found out that age and sex are determining factors in shaping positive attitudes toward homosexuality, with increasing young adults and women being more open to LGBTQI rights and culture compared to men and earlier generations. Additional factors contributing to positive attitudes include greater levels of education, and one's affiliation to political parties with an orientation toward the left wing.

The comparison of these international findings with those of Eurispes (2020), a private research institute analyzing the ongoing cultural shifts on the Italian territory through the investigation of changes in citizens' attitudes and opinions toward particular thematic issues, is of interest when examining the effects of the implementation of Law 76/2016 on the online discourses and attitudes of Italian publics. Four years after its enactment, 63.1 percent of women interviewed by Eurispes are reported to be in favor of same-sex marriage, while 55.8 percent of males were against it. Investigating further the population segment, the majority of those in favor of same-sex marriage (77.1 percent) include individuals between 18–24 years of age (+17 percent compared to the data from 2019), followed by those aged 25–34 years (70.1 percent), 35–44 years of age (66.2 percent), 45–64 years of age (55.7 percent) and over 64 years of age (45.3 percent). Even when it comes to the possibility of LGBT couples adopting children, the study shows that 55.1 percent of women are reported to be far more in favor than 61 percent of men.

Analyzing geographies of intolerance

LGBTQI activists in Italy expressed general consensus that it may be too soon to assess whether a real change in public attitudes has taken place after the enactment of Law 76/2016. As Mario di Martino, former Vice President of MIT, argued, each political gain has its rising conflicts (interview on 28 October 2020). Valuable sites for the exploration of these conflicts are the maps of intolerance produced by the Vox Observatory on Human Rights in collaboration with the Statale University in Milan, Aldo Moro University in Bari, Sapienza University in Rome and Cattolica University in Milan. Created during the period 2014–2020 with the objective of tracking online hate speech spreading across the Italian territory and identifying the groups most targeted by this hate (women, homosexuals, migrants, people with disabilities, Jews, and Muslims), a qualitative media analysis of these "geographies of intolerance" enables us to assess the shifts in online hate speech discourse and attitudes that have taken place prior to and after the enactment of the civil union's law.

In the first map of intolerance (2014), misogyny and violent discourse against women were the most prominent on Twitter, followed by antisemitism, homophobia, racism and discrimination against people with disabilities. A common thread in the hate propagated against these target groups is the discursive power to construct subjectivities through offenses that are, on one hand, almost always framed to dehumanize the body – sexualized, mutilated, deformed, mortified, inferior, violated; on the other hand, obsessive references to feces are used to render the abject body impure and contaminated, further emphasizing distance and rejection of the Other. The second map of intolerance shows that between August 2015 and February 2016, homophobic discourse was the most prominent on Twitter, followed by antisemitism, racism, disability, misogyny and islamophobia. Rome, Milan, Naples and Bologna were identified as the most homophobic cities in Italy. The peak of online homophobic speech was recorded concomitantly to several events: the dispute between Roberto Mancini, Inter's soccer coach and Maurizio Sarri, Naples' coach during the Coppa Italia game; Valerio Scanu's participation during the Sanremo Music Festival, and discussions in the Senate on the passing of the civil union's law. Interestingly, when comparing the results of this map (prior to the enactment of the civil unions law), with the map of intolerance issued in 2019, the evidence shows that during the period of March–May 2019, the dissemination of homophobic discourse dramatically dropped in the rankings, with xenophobia and antisemitism now at the top. Instances of online hate speech reached their peak mainly during debates on rainbow families and during the Verona World Congress of Families.

Are legal means enough to combat hate?

The position of several LGBTQI actors as well as the Vox Observatory on Human Rights is that initiatives and campaigns spearheaded by a stronger and more unified LGBTQI Italian movement in the years leading up to the passing of the law notably contributed to shaping public consciousness and promoting more favorable attitudes and perceptions toward the LGBTQI community, both offline and online. Moreover, the enactment of the law increased visibility and representations of the LGBT community, including in the mainstream media, and educational and awareness-raising programs played a key role in promoting a cultural shift and diminishing online hate. This is also reflected in the latest map of intolerance published in 2020, which reports an overall decline in homophobic online discourse, with the exception of instances where the Zan Bill against homotransphobia was under discussion in Parliament.

Consistent with Flores and Barclay's (2016) Legitimacy Model and Aksoy et al.'s (2018) evidence from same-sex relationship recognition policies in Europe, laws do cause changes in attitudes, hence the indisputable importance of their enforcement. Respondents of the EU-LGBTI II Survey from EU member states who have reported a decrease in prejudice, intolerance and violence in their countries, also clearly identified the importance of "positive changes in law and policy" and "support by public figures, community leaders and civil society" as determinant factors in the improvement of societal attitudes towards LGBTQI people (EU FRA, 2020, p. 13). However, as peace and conflict theorists would argue, enforcing laws is just one step forward. To eradicate hate and move toward a long-term positive peace, one where harmony, justice, equity, empathy, and respect of human rights would be the leading values in societies, it is essential to understand and address the dynamics and underlying root causes of conflicts. As Johan Galtung (1996) reminds us, peace is not the absence of conflict, it is rather the absence of violence. This violence can be expressed physically (direct violence), through dominant systems of oppression and subordination (structural violence), or through the ideological use of cultural products (cultural violence), more than ever disseminated through and within the media. All three forms are interrelated and mutually reinforcing. Hence, discrimination, hate, intolerance, homophobia, xenophobia, racism, sexism, misogyny, prejudice will not be eradicated by laws alone. Changing people's attitudes and behaviors, and ultimately attaining positive peace, will require a deep transformation in both the institutions and the discourses that reproduce violence. Counter-action, strengthening institutional systems to combat hate speech and hate crime, policies on social inclusion, restorative justice measures, reconciliation efforts and promoting a culture of human rights are critical and necessary to eradicate and heal hate.

Hate speech regulatory frameworks

Hate speech and hate crimes are a threat to human rights – civil, political, economic, social and collective. They are also an obstacle to attaining peace, security and social stability. No society is spared from hate, but the ways in which states decide to deal with the latter will indeed have an impact on the degree of how much hate will spread, be mitigated or contained. In the European Union, member states apply different standards to regulate and counteract hate speech and hate crimes, some more effectively than others. Hate speech on social media is addressed at the European level through the non-legally binding *EU Code of Conduct on Countering Illegal Hate Speech Online* (2020). Moreover, in 2020, the European Parliament adopted two resolutions on the basis of Article 225 of the Treaty on the Functioning of the European Union (TFEU): the Digital Services Act – Improving the Functioning of the Single Market and the Digital Services Act – Adapting Commercial and Civil Law Rules for Commercial Entities Operating Online. These resolutions are complementary and are a call to action to protect fundamental rights in the online environment, ensuring transparency, fairness, information obligations and account-ability for digital service providers, and advocating for effective obli-gations to tackle illegal content online.

The Organization for Security and Co-operation in Europe's (OSCE) Office for Democratic Institutions and Human Rights (ODIHR) pro-vides support, assistance and expertise to participating states and civil society to promote democracy, rule of law, human rights, tolerance and non-discrimination, with particular attention to the monitoring and reporting of hate crimes. Several recommendations to member states have also been provided by the Committee of Ministers of the Council of Europe, tackling hate speech, media and the promotion of a culture of tolerance (Rec (97) 20, Rec (97) 21, 1997). Recommendation CM/Rec (2010) 5 on measures to combat discrimination on the grounds of sexual orientation or gender identity is of particular relevance in that it clearly includes member states' obligation to combat hate crimes and hate speech against LGBTI+ people, including in the media and on the Internet:

> Member states should take appropriate measures to combat all forms of expression, including in the media and on the Inter-net, which may be reasonably understood as likely to produce the effect of inciting, spreading or promoting hatred or other forms of discrimination against lesbian, gay, bisexual and transgender persons. Such "hate speech" should be prohibited and publicly disavowed whenever it occurs. All measures should respect the fundamental right to freedom of expression in accordance with Article 10 of the Convention and the case law of the Court.
>
> (Council of Europe, 2010, CM/Rec 5)

On a global scale, in 2018 UN Secretary-General Antonio Guterres launched the *United Nations Strategy and Plan of Action on Hate Speech* with the aim of enhancing UN efforts to address root causes and drivers of hate speech, and enable effective UN responses to the impact of hate speech on societies (United Nations, 2019). This Plan of Action presupposes the right to freedom of opinion and expression as key means to addressing hate speech and keeping the latter from escalating into something more dangerous such as incitement to discrimination, hostility and violence, which is prohibited under international law (ibid.). Media, technology and advocacy are listed as key commitments for addressing and countering hate speech, including through the promotion of strengthened partnerships between government, industry, social media companies, and civil society.

The Italian scenario

In the past two decades, Italy has experienced a significant rise in the number of recorded episodes of hate crime and incitement to hatred against individuals based on ethnic, racial, religious, and sexual grounds. Arcigay monitoring reports show that, from 2006–2020, there has been an increase in the number of homotransphobic acts (both physical and using discriminatory language mainly on social media), in spite of national and international existing laws, policies and regulatory frameworks in place (Steri, 2020). The majority of cases were recorded during 2016–2017 (196 cases), with decreasing numbers in 2018 (119). In 2019, however, the number of homotransphobic acts newly went up (187). Forced isolation due to COVID-19 restrictions must also not be underestimated as many who have become vulnerable to homelessness during the pandemic were forced to move back into hostile family and community situations. Data from Italy's Gay Center gayhelpline.it shows that in 2020 one person out of three (36.7 percent) reported to have been victim of discrimination, homophobic aggressions and violence within the household. Within the population under 18 years of age, 39.85 percent reported having been exposed to homophobic violence inflicted by their parents, with the highest victims (52.08 percent) being trans people. As Arcigay further reports, during the period 2019–2020, homotransphobic acts mainly manifested in the form of aggressions, incitement to discrimination and insults, and political speech fueling discrimination and intolerance (which, as seen earlier in this section, are prohibited under international law) (ibid.).

This was reconfirmed in ILGA-Europe's (2021) Annual Review of the Human Rights Situation of Lesbian, Gay, Bisexual, Trans and

Intersex People in Europe and Central Asia, which highlights two particular instances of bias-motivated speech. In August, a member of the Rome City Council, Massimiliano Quaresima stated at a meeting that "homosexuality is a disease and is caused by vaccines." In July, one of Vercelli's city councilors was sentenced to four months' probation and a 3,000 euro fine for his social media post saying, "kill lesbians, gays, and pedophiles." While abuse and hate speech against LGBTQI people is on the rise, particularly online, ILGA-Europe has also observed that more people are turning to the courts for the recognition of their human rights, or for the clarification of existing legislation that is meant to protect them. In Italy, however, 70 percent of LGBTI people think the government is not effectively combating hate, prejudice and intolerance toward the community (EU FRA, 2020). The absence of a law that would protect people from homo-transphobia leads to under-reporting and under-recording of homo-transphobic violent acts, pushing further away the prospects of peace, justice, equality and security.

The role of the National Anti-racial Discrimination Office (UNAR)

Strategies for dialogue between LGBT organizations and the National Anti-racial Discrimination Office (UNAR), the national specialized body in the fight against racism and intolerance have been established and strengthened over the years, but the latter is not entitled to take legal actions to combat discrimination. Set up within the Department for Equal Opportunities under the Presidency of the Council of Ministers (Article 7 of Legislative Decree 215/2003 pursuant to European Council Directive 2000/43/EC), UNAR uses a systemic approach to combating discrimination on the basis of sexual orientation and gender identity, one based on prevention, awareness-raising, removal and counteraction of prejudice and stereotypes. However, as Agnese Canevari, Head of the Office, explained (2021), most victims of violence and discrimination do not directly report their cases through UNAR's contact center. The number of institutionalized discrimination cases being reported to UNAR are higher than individual discrimination cases. Hence, building a strong network with organizations working on the ground, at the territorial level, is of critical importance since these are victims' first point of contact. In spite of the fact that 66 LGBT actors have joined UNAR's roundtables, working groups, and consultations, and are currently providing input on the priorities that will be included in the new National LGBT Strategy, several semi-periphery and periphery actors reported being skeptical about the effectiveness and inclusiveness of UNAR's work. Some have argued core actors are those who most of the times are being awarded funds and consulted, as opposed to more peripheral, territorial and marginal realities. In addition, while Cammini di Speranza has joined UNAR's roundtables, faith actors reported their thematic issues are greatly under-represented in roundtable discussions.

If challenges persist in multi-stakeholder community organizing and partnerships building, it is also true that opportunities exist for greater synergies to take place among LGBT actors. Placed at the intersection of a network that coordinates actions between national and local LGBT organizations, civil society organizations, international, European and intergovernmental organizations (including the Council of Europe, the European Commission and the United Nations), UNAR has the opportunity to play a key role in supporting LGBT mobilizations. This could be done, for example, through a fair and equal distribution of resources, funds and information, leaving no one behind, as well as through a more bottom-up collaborative planning and co-creation of activities spanning across thematic issues. Agnese Canevari agreed that the exchange of good practices from LGBT actors is of key importance, yet currently not enough is being showcased and exchanged. Substantial work is being done to promote and protect human rights and fight discrimination, but the dominant narratives that are being mainstreamed nationally and transnationally (more than ever through social media) are always centered on haters and politicians' hate speech discourses rather than on LGBT peace activists and their achievements. This is sending the wrong message to the world that Italy is a country of haters and homophobes, when in reality haters are not representatives of the whole Italian population.

Platforms such as the National Portal for LGBT Information and Non-discrimination (currently being re-developed) can greatly contribute to strengthening the Italian LGBT movement's identity and voice as one more cohesive and united (both nationally and transnationally, including in political arenas). Currently, however, no platform or database systematically and effectively gathers: information and contacts of LGBTQI actors working across thematic issues, existing campaigns, initiatives and case studies (including at the territorial level), toolkits and capacity-building materials developed for LGBT activists, updated national research, reports and surveys, among others. Even though this information is invisible it does not necessarily mean that it does not exist. As the national focal point on LGBT issues, UNAR is required to have a stronger organizational communication strategy in place. This will be key in establishing a better two-way communication with LGBT activists and increasing their motivation to collaboratively contribute to the implementation of the new LGBT National Strategy.

New advocacy priorities for the protection of LGBTQI rights

Initially approved on 4 November 2020 by Italy's lower house of parliament, and ultimately rejected on 27 October 2021 by Italy's upper house Senate, the focus of Italian LGBTQI activists' advocacy efforts and discourses is centered on the passing of the Zan Bill to prevent and combat discrimination and violence on the grounds of sex, gender, sexual orientation, gender identity and disability. While marriage equality has not been achieved yet and online discourses on this issue have decreased both on social media and online news compared to five years ago, Michele Albiani, Representative of the Rights Department at the Democratic Party Milano Metropolitana, explained during a workshop on "Advocacy and Planning: Tools for the LGBTQI+ Community," in April 2021 that the advocacy that has taken place during the years leading to the passing of the law on civil unions is greatly inspiring the digital media activism practices the democratic party is using today to advocate for the passing of the Zan Bill. Facebook was crucial in the popularization of the Cirinnà law, as were a full range of applications such as Telegram, WhatsApp, Messenger, but also social networking and online dating applications for LGBTQI+ people such as grindr and Romeo. All these channels are being used by activists to build their "tribe," mobilizing action, strengthening networks and bringing Italian activists together to discuss the issues at stake.

In addition to social media, guerrilla activism tactics and email bombing initiatives such as #RinvioNonFico ("postponing not cool") launched on Instagram by Albiani, renowned celebrity influencers such as Chiara Ferragni and her husband Fedez are also playing their part in putting pressure on politicians. During an Instagram live-stream with Alessandro Zan, Fedez invited over 30,000 connected followers to sign the petition and send an email to Senator Andrea Ostellari, President of the Justice Committee of the Senate, not to postpone the discussion and approval of the bill. His appeals continued during a music concert that took place on 1 May, where the rapper publicly condemned on national television those who oppose the Zan Bill, calling out politicians who have stood out for their homophobic discourses. Indeed, social media are increasingly being used by LGBTQI activists and allies as strong political militancy tools, and some may even argue for "pinkwashing," in other words, transforming resistance into consumption and promoting a particular corporate or political agenda. It is precisely at this stage that we witness the impacts of social movements on culture, and those of cultural resistance on contentious politics. However, as Valerio Colamasi Battaglia, President of the Circolo di Cultura Omosessuale Mario Mieli, noted in 2021, increased digital media activism has at the same time resulted in activists' increased disengagement in physical mobilizations (also due to the pandemic). Striking the right balance between online and offline participatory action is important.

The Zan Bill: a catalyst for social change

When a state does not stand up to combat hate, racism, discrimination, intolerance, exclusions (structural and institutionalized violence), then it gives a license to other actors to engage in violent homophobic, discriminatory, and racist behavior and go unpunished. As Monica Cirinnà has stated:

> To understand the need and the urgency of a good law on misogyny and homotransphobia it is sufficient to look around, open the pages of a newspaper, or more simply speak to the victims of discrimination and hate. We urgently need this law because Italy needs to strengthen the culture of equality and respect towards the other, and this can only happen by punishing hate and violence, while also promoting tangible actions on the cultural level and supporting victims. This is exactly what the Zan Bill does: prevent, counteract and support.
>
> (in Foderi, 2020)

Structured into ten articles, the highly debated Zan Bill on measures to prevent and counteract discrimination and violence on the basis of sex, gender, sexual orientation, gender identity, and disability, proposes an amendment of Articles 604-bis and 604-ter of the penal code. The first six articles are concerned with enforcing harsher penalties for hate perpetrators; retributive justice is only the tip of the iceberg. The remaining four articles outline positive actions to counteract discrimination (including a 4 million euros fund to invest in educational and awareness-raising initiatives in schools) with a long-term vision to create an enabling environment for tolerance, inclusion and equality to thrive.

While much of the attention and weight has been directed toward retributive justice, the punitive measures of the bill, and misleading accusations on limitations of freedom of expression, it is arguably articles 7–10 that hold the promise and the true potential of the legislation to facilitate a cultural shift and behavioral change in discriminatory and homophobic attitudes toward the LGBTQI community, as well as toward people with disabilities. Bayer and Bárd (2020) maintain:

> Restorative justice (RJ) techniques could be employed to deal with hate crimes, with special regard to the fact that there are deep-rooted social conflicts behind these actions. It is insufficient to focus only on the actual crime. In addition to establishing individual responsibility, the tensions between communities shall be addressed, and restorative justice, the goal of which is restoring social justice, could be an ideal tool.
>
> (p. 108)

Viewing crime as a violation of people and relationships is central to the concept of restorative justice (Zehr, 1990). While there is no normative definition of the latter, for Elizabeth Kiss (2000), restorative justice includes the threefold commitment:

> [To] affirm and restore the dignity of those whose human rights have been violated; hold perpetrators accountable, emphasizing the harm that they have done to individual human beings; and create social conditions in which human rights will be respected.
>
> (p. 79)

The main difference between restorative and retributive justice lies in the former's commitment to "correcting imbalances, restoring broken relationships – with healing, harmony and reconciliation" (Tutu, 1998, p. 9). The concerns, goals and values of restorative justice: dignity, equality, non-discrimination, respect, harmony and well-being, among others, are the foundation of democratic, peaceful and just societies. These are also enshrined in the Italian Constitution and international human rights treaties, to which Italy is a signatory.

Hence, as Alessandro Zan has expressed multiple times, there is no justification for right-wing political parties and conservative Catholics to obstruct the passing of this law. This law was not created to be used by political parties as an ideological flag for mobilizing support, exacerbating divisions, and reinforcing us-versus-them narratives. It was conceived, on the other hand, as an opportunity for the country to have in place a legal framework tackling both retributive and restorative justice measures to enable institutions to protect the most vulnerable victims of discrimination, intolerance and hate. The development of a National Strategy for the prevention and counteraction of discrimination based on sexual orientation and gender identity was also expected to be led by UNAR if the bill were approved. Cooperation by the police, prosecutors' offices, judiciary, victims' services and civil society organizations would also have been critical in order to fulfill the promises of this law. Of equal importance would have been mainstreaming knowledge and narratives of democracy, peace, human rights, and tolerance through media and cultural institutions. LGBTQI organizations are ready to take on the roles and responsibilities needed for the transition toward a more inclusive society. With the future approval of the Zan Bill, there would be a regulatory framework that would have enabled these organizations to more effectively educate youths and collaborate with teachers in formal and non-formal educational settings, assist journalists and media professionals in gender-sensitive reporting, promote the values of diversity and inclusion in the private sector and enterprises, ultimately advocating more strongly and safely for LGBTQI equality.

Conclusion

Through the analysis of the geographies of intolerance, this chapter has shown that policy achievements and regulatory frameworks are important in catalyzing more favorable public attitudes and behaviors toward LGBT people, both online and offline. This was reinforced by evidence from 2019 and 2020, where the dissemination of online homophobic discourse on social media dramatically decreased after the enactment of Law 76/2016 on civil unions. However, the recent new wave of hate crime and incitement to hatred against sexual minorities in Italy is a strong signal that laws alone are not enough to bring about social change. To eradicate hate and move toward a long-term positive peace, a deep transformation in both the institutions and the discourses that reproduce violence will be required. Counter-action, strengthening institutional systems to combat hate speech and hate crime, policies on social inclusion, restorative justice measures, and widely promoting a culture of human rights and peace through digital media and counter-hate speech discourses are fundamental. Moreover, fostering better partnerships and collaborations among activists and stakeholders working toward the achievement of common and shared social justice goals is also a necessity. Against this backdrop, the Zan Bill, one that includes both retributive and restorative justice measures, is timely and necessary. Not only will this law protect minorities and vulnerable people, and bring hate perpetrators to justice. It will also set a plan of action for the transition to a culture of acceptance, tolerance and equality.

Notes

1 Article 19 of ICCPR states:

1 Everyone shall have the right to hold opinions without interference.
2 Everyone shall have the right to freedom of expression; this right shall include freedom to seek, receive and impart information and ideas of all kinds, regardless of frontiers, either orally, in writing or in print, in the form of art, or through any other media of his choice.
3 The exercise of the rights provided for in paragraph 2 of this article carries with it special duties and responsibilities. It may therefore be subject to certain restrictions, but these shall only be such as are provided by law and are necessary:

   a For respect of the rights or reputations of others;
   b For the protection of national security or public order (*ordre public*), or of public health or morals.

2 Article 10 provides that:

1 Everyone has the right to freedom of expression. This right shall include freedom to hold opinions and to receive and impart information and ideas without interference by public authority and regardless of frontiers. This Article shall not prevent States from requiring the licensing of broadcasting, television, or cinema enterprises.
2 The exercise of these freedoms, since it carries with it duties and responsibilities, may be subject to such formalities, conditions, restrictions or penalties as are prescribed by law and are necessary in a democratic society, in the interests of national security, territorial integrity or public safety, for the prevention of disorder or crime, for the protection of health or morals, for the protection of the reputation or rights of others, for preventing the disclosure of information received in confidence, or for maintaining the authority and impartiality of the judiciary.

3 L. 76/2016, Article 1(2).
4 L. 76/2016, Article 1(4).
5 L. 76/2016, Article 1 (5–7).
6 L. 76/2016, Article 1 (11).

References

Albiani, M. (2021) Online workshop. Pianificazione operativa di progetti per le comunità Advocacy e progettazione: strumenti per la comunità LGBTQI+.

ILGA Europe and Advocacy Rainbow Coalition, 28 April.Article 19 (2013) Traditional values? Attempts to censor sexuality. Homosexual propaganda bans, freedom of expression and equality. Available at: https://www.article19. org/data/files/medialibrary/3637/LGBT-propaganda-report-ENGLISH.pdf.

Askoy, C.G., Carpenter, C.S., De Haas, R., and Tran, K. (2018) Do laws shape attitudes? Evidence from same-sex relationship recognition policies in Europe. IZA Institute of Labor Economics. Available at: https://www.iza. org/en/publications/dp/11743/do-laws-shape-attitudes-evidence-from-sam e-sex-relationship-recognition-policies-in-europe.

Ayoub, P.M., and Garretson, J. (2017) Getting the message out: Media context and global changes in attitudes toward homosexuality. *Comparative Political Studies*, 50 (8), 1055–1085. https://doi.org/10.1177/001041401666683.

Bayer, J., and Bárd, P. (2020) Hate speech and hate crime in the EU and the evaluation of online content regulation approaches, Brussels: Policy Department for Citizen's Rights and Constitutional Affairs European Parliament, European Union.

Canevari, A. (2021) Online workshop. Pianificazione operativa di progetti per le comunità Advocacy e progrettazione: strumenti per la comunità LGBTQI +. ILGA Europe and Advocacy Rainbow Coalition, 28 April.

Colamasi Battaglia, V. (2021) Online workshop. Pianificazione operativa di progetti per le comunità Advocacy e progrettazione: strumenti per la comunità LGBTQI+. ILGA Europe and Advocacy Rainbow Coalition, 28 April.

Council of Europe (2010) Recommendation CM/Rec (2010) 5 of the Committee of Ministers to member states on measures to combat discrimination on grounds of sexual orientation or gender identity. Available at: https://www. coe.int/en/web/sogi/rec-2010-5.

EU FRA (European Union Agency for Fundamental Right) (2020) A long way to go for LGBTI equality, Publications Office of the European Union. Available at: https://fra.europa.eu/en/publication/2020/eu-lgbti-survey-results.

Eurispes (2020) 32a Edizione Rapporto Italia 2020. EURISPES Istituto di Studi Politici Economici e Sociali.

Flores, A.R., and Barclay, S. (2016) Backlash, consensus, legitimacy, or polarization: The effect of same-sex marriage policy on mass attitudes, *Political Research Quarterly*, 69 (1): 43–56.

Foderi, A. (2020) Perché l'Italia ha bisogno di una legge sull'omotransfobia. Available at: https://www.wired.it/attualita/politica/2020/06/23/omofobia-ita lia-legge-zan/.

Galtung, J. (1996) *Peace by Peaceful Means: Peace and Conflict, Development and Civilization*, London: Sage Publications.

Gay Help Line (2020) LGBT+ e isolamento COVID-19. Available at: gayhelp line.it.

ILGA-Europe (2021) Human rights situation of Lesbian, Gay, Bisexual, Trans and Intersex people in Europe and Central Asia. Available at: https://www. ilga-europe.org/annualreview/2021.

Kiss, E. (2000) Moral ambition within and beyond political constraints: Reflections on restorative justice, in R.I. Rotberg and D. Thompson (Eds.), *Truth v, Justice: The Morality of Truth Commissions*, Princeton, NJ: Princeton University Press, pp. 68–98.

La Rue, F. (2011) Report of the Special Rapporteur on the promotion and protection of the right to freedom of opinion and expression, 17th session, Human Rights Council. Available at: https://www2.ohchr.org/english/bodies/hrcouncil/docs/17session/a.hrc.17.27_en.pdf.

Pew Research Center (2020) The global divide on homosexuality persists. Available at: https://www.pewresearch.org/global/wp-content/uploads/sites/2/2020/06/PG_2020.06.25_Global-Views-Homosexuality_FINAL.pdf.

Redman, S.M. (2018) Effects of same-sex legislation on attitudes toward homosexuality, *Political Research Quarterly*, 71 (3), 628–641. https://doi.org/10.1177/1065912917753077.

Steri, E. (2020) Legge Zan: necessaria o liberticida? L'omofobia spiegata attraverso i numeri, Available at: datajournalism.it.

Tutu, D. (1998) Chairperson's Foreword, in *Truth and Reconciliation Commission of South Africa Report*, vol. 1. Available at: https://www.justice.gov.za/trc/report/finalreport/Volume%201.pdf.

United Nations (1948) Universal Declaration on Human Rights. Available at: https://www.un.org/en/about-us/universal-declaration-of-human-rights.

United Nations (2019) United Nations Strategy and Plan of Action on Hate Speech. Available at: https://www.un.org/en/genocideprevention/documents/advising-and-mobilizing/Action_plan_on_hate_speech_EN.pdf.

Vox Observatory on Human Rights (2019) The maps of intolerance. Available at: http://www.voxdiritti.it/la-nuova-mappa-dellintolleranza-4/.

Winkler, M.M. (2017) Italy's gentle revolution: The new law on same-sex partnerships, *National Italian American Bar Association Law Journal*, 1 (25): 1–31.

Zehr, H. (1990) *Changing Lenses: A New Focus for Crime and Justice*, Scottsdale, PA: Herald Press.

7 Conclusion

Rendering visible LGBTQI cultural resistance, expressed through digital media activism and counter-hate discourse is of the utmost importance not only in Italy but also globally. Invisibility and the symbolic annihilation of LGBTQI people in media and popular discourse have historically signified powerlessness for LGBTQI people, and have also contributed to the dissemination of harmful misrepresentations of gender and LGBTQI identities, promoting negative stereotyping, increasing prejudices, hate, discrimination and homophobia, also leading to direct physical violence in many cases. These attitudes are fully embodied and expressed by actors mobilizing nationally and transnationally in anti-gender countermovements.

Following movement-countermovement dynamics, granting rights to LGBTQI people in Europe created a demand for conservative counteractions that ultimately resulted in an increase of constitutional bans on same-sex marriage, anti-LGBTI politics, and the spreading of anti-gender mobilizations. In Italy, the Catholic Church has played a critical role in the emergence and the development of gender ideology and the Theory of Gender, carefully defining and legitimizing narrative discourses on normalized sexuality, acceptable biological behavior and gender norms. An analysis of the actors and networks involved in Italian anti-gender mobilizations was presented in order to understand the ideological matrix of these mobilizations, their tactics and repertories of action, and their intersection with populist right political projects. Even though the Italian anti-gender countermovement has tried to boycott and create a backlash on LGBTQI equality, it has at the same time contributed to raising the public profile of human rights and key issues that are relevant to LGBTQI people. The latter has furthermore generated an increased media interest in issues, such as same-sex marriage equality, civil unions, rainbow families, among others, gaining the attention of policy-makers, both nationally and

DOI: 10.4324/9781003289951-7

transnationally. In Italy, anti-gender mobilizations have also pushed activists to build alliances and networks with other movements beyond the LGBTQI community, strengthening their legitimacy and recognition.

While a great amount of scholarship has been invested in studying anti-gender mobilizations and their violent and trauma-generating discourses, this book has shifted the attention to LGBTQI social movements and their digital media activism and non-violent communication practices. The extensive literature review that was carried out also shed light on an interesting fact. Italian scholars have most of the time addressed in their research the "negatives," in other words, the dominant discourses of oppression and subordination, and the actors perpetrating hate, homophobia and discrimination. Those who are working to improve the prospects of peace, justice and equality for LGBTQI people, building and strengthening communities, and producing uplifting and healing effects through their work, are almost entirely neglected or invisible. The research presented in this book aimed to fill this gap by reclaiming the voice and experiences of the Italian periphery, semi-periphery and core activists working across identified key thematic clusters (multi-issues, culture and education, family, faith and homosexuality) and rendering their voices not only visible but also loud.

Major findings on digital media use and capacity of LGBTQI activists

The value of using digital and social media in NGOs and volunteering associations' strategic communication practices has been recognized by all the actors involved in this research, particularly during the COVID-19 pandemic. In this challenging context, Italian activists have rethought how best to support the LGBTQI community through digital media and outreach efforts. They have also invested in their internal and external communication infrastructure in order to continue their political, cultural and social activities at a distance. Webinars, Facebook live events, online political labs, film screenings, web TV broadcasting sessions, book presentations, assistance and psychological support, online campaigns advocating for the passing of the Zan Bill, and developing digital contents to raise awareness on LGBTQI issues and rights, are among the most prominent activities conducted by LGBTQI organizations in Italy. Furthermore, migrating activities online had a multiplier effect. It opened new opportunities for scaling-up actions and strengthening nationally the voice of local networks.

Paradoxically, the pandemic, the increased use of easily accessible digital media platforms, and the variety of thematic issues discussed during online webinars, have also enabled organizations to indirectly reach more diverse audiences. The participation of non-LGBTQI activists, representatives of feminist movements, disability rights activists, among others has opened a window of opportunity for more intersectional interventions and cross-fertilization of discourses.

Accountability mechanisms

When asked about their biggest online security and safety concerns and whether organizations ensure their media work is accountable to their community members, all actors reported having some sort of mechanism in place. For example, all organizations usually request written or verbal consent to use community members' stories, videos and testimonies. Furthermore, to avoid attracting haters and trolls on their platforms, organizations review contents and consult with their board members before posting on social media. While there is a strong awareness of the dangers and risks of gender-based violence, hate speech, stalking, and discrimination against LGBTQI people, based on information revealed in their social media profiles and posts, all actors expressed their confidence about their cautious content development practices and reported they were not overly concerned about issues of security and safety.

Key challenges and gaps

Many organizations still struggle when it comes to developing and implementing effective communication strategies and plans that will enable them to reach their organizational goals. None reported having an official written communication and social media strategy or plan in place. Moreover, communications is not only never budgeted for in financial plans as a stand-alone activity, but also is never recognized as paid work for internal staff members or volunteers. The organizational communication of Italian non-governmental organizations is still greatly undervalued and underfunded, consequently also hindering the development of much-needed capacity building programs.

In most cases, volunteers with no communications background and training, including Presidents and Executive Board members, are charged with organizational communication responsibilities, including: ensuring the appropriate visibility of their organization on multiple media channels, social media management, reaching out to the community to increase membership, creating and disseminating news, events, information and services, planning social media campaigns, fundraising, and creating safe spaces for community storytelling to take place. While most of the work is done internally, several actors also hire external communication agencies to work on specific projects and initiatives. The generational digital divide was also identified as an obstacle to effective media activism and advocacy, especially in organizations run by parents or activists of older generations.

Reaching mainstream media to improve LGBTQI coverage and advocacy was also identified as one of the main challenges. The majority of organizations do not have a list of media and press contacts. All acknowledged, however, that a first step toward improving the coverage of the LGBTQI community and preventing hate speech and violent discourse would be for mainstream journalists to use accurate and respectful language and terminology. Capacity building of journalists and media professionals on gender-sensitive reporting is necessary and must not occur in a silo, distant from front-line actors operating within the LGBTQI community. Where personal relationships between journalists and activists have been established, more attention and care have been addressed to accurate gender-sensitive reporting. Face-to-face communication remains of fundamental importance in building relationships with journalists and allies, as well as in community organizing and movement building.

Major findings on media and communication priorities of LGBTQI actors

While all the organizations identified LGBTQI community members as the primary target audience of their organizational communication strategies and practices, the importance of not leaving out the general public, as well as European publics, was also emphasized by the actors. If media experts are aware of the value and importance of a digital presence, non-governmental organizations (NGOs), civil society organizations (CSOs) and associations of volunteers are also increasingly recognizing that the first (online) impression matters! As a result of this research and the interviews conducted with key Italian LGBTQI organizations, the following priority impact categories emerged. These vary greatly across actors, and in some cases, also within an organization itself. There was a general consensus that having a digital footprint is crucial when:

- establishing authority and legitimacy of an organization, at local, national and transnational levels, and among stakeholders from multiple sectors;
- strengthening branding and the identity of one's organization, projects, initiatives or events, and boosting visibility across media channels and platforms;
- ensuring credibility and reliability, particularly during fundraising activities, donation requests, increasing membership, mobilizing resources across national, European and global networks;
- building and strengthening communities, especially during the COVID-19 lockdown, where digital media was crucial in maintaining ties and building a sense of community and belonging among LGBTQI people in lockdown, as well as those residing in remote rural areas in the South and the North of Italy;
- building partnerships and networks to strengthen social movements, gaining supporters and allies for one's cause, initiating conversations with community members, delivering organizations' knowledge and services, reaching targeted beneficiaries;
- coordinating movement's mobilizations. Increasingly, social media, particularly Facebook and Instagram, are being used in online mobilizations, almost entirely replacing traditional forms of collective action, for instance, gathering in public squares and joining street protests (which have been impossible during the pandemic). Social media platforms are also being used to express political opinions, getting policy-makers to pay attention to LGBTQI issues, and influencing policy decisions.
- communicating experience, telling stories, mainstreaming accurate representations of LGBTQI people, promoting counter-hate speech and human rights discourses.

Lessons learnt and insights from the Advocacy and Planning Workshop

In April–May 2021, I had the opportunity to attend a five-day workshop on "Advocacy and Planning: Tools for the LGBTQI+ Community," organized by ILGA Europe and the Advocacy Rainbow Coalition, facilitated by the Quore organization. Attending this course greatly enriched and strengthened my research findings. It also introduced me to many more periphery, semi-periphery and core actors working at national and territorial levels, all interacting with each other online. Guest speakers who led the courses included social worker and activist Dr. Deborah Di Cave, who provided key insights on the "archeology" of the Italian LGBT movement, and the shifts in discourses and claims that have taken place since the organization of the first official Pride in 1994. Alessio Garbin, Digital Marketing Manager working at Edge, the first group of LGBTI+ entrepreneurs, managers, professionals and their allies in Italy, conducted the session on "communications for the community." The importance of having in place a written strategy and plan of action when conducting advocacy and communication activities was stressed. In line with the findings presented in this book, the majority of workshop participants reported not having such written strategies in place. Valerio Colamasi Battaglia, President of the Circolo di Cultura Omosessuale Mario Mieli, further explained that a written plan of action will serve as a key tool for transparency and accountability, and will be critical in the monitoring and evaluation of organizational activities and the attainment of identified goals (in the short, medium and long term).

Giulio Mariotti, from Omphalos, focused instead on techniques for participatory action and motivational strategies to boost activists' engagement. Most trainers reported a decrease in participatory activism within the LGBTQI community, particularly among youths. The strong generational gap among activists and their diversity of visions, mobilization practices and approaches were also emphasized. Participants expressed the importance of valuing the past but also becoming more forward-looking and embracing innovation. Moreover, the importance of non-violent communications (especially in counteracting hate speech) was highlighted. Currently, however, there is a lack of capacity-building programs tackling peace and non-violent communications among NGOs and within schools, reported Mariotti. Finally, the contribution of Dr. Agnese Canevari, Head of UNAR, provided a more institutionalized perspective on national projects and initiatives targeting the LGBTQI community, including ongoing consultations to develop the new National LGBT Strategy. This contribution shed light on the importance for UNAR to strengthen social dialogues and relationships with grassroots organizations working at the local and territorial levels. The lower level of engagement and interaction during this session (compared to the others) was also a sign that activists, in particular, youths, could not easily relate to institutionalized figures. More inclusive spaces should be created where national, territorial and local networks can informally come together, share good practices and collaboratively plan for the implementation of coordinated activities.

UNAR is also a key actor in the mobilization of national and European funds allocated to initiatives to prevent and counteract discrimination. In addition to public funds, non-profits in Italy are increasingly reaching out to individuals, private foundations and enterprises in their fundraising activities. The use of crowdfunding platforms is becoming more popular alongside more traditional fundraising methods, such as the organization of events, the 5x1000, sponsorships, using emails and newsletters and investing in advertising (online and offline). However, most LGBTQI actors (core, semi-periphery, and periphery) have not yet mastered the fundraising communications skills needed to effectively reach out to donors, tell their stories powerfully and successfully raise funds for their organizations. Beyond the "Strategic Communications Framing Equality Toolkit" (2017), developed by ILGA-Europe and the Public Interest Research Centre (in English), to guide activists and campaigners in developing their communications for social change strategies and contents, there are very limited practical, appealing, context- and culture-sensitive resources for Italian activists. For semi-periphery and periphery actors, not mastering these skills is equivalent to not having a fair shot in the race for the allocation of resources or, not being able to secure a seat at roundtables where the co-planning of initiatives are being discussed. Moreover, lack of strong networking skills with businesses, enterprises and the private sector has also been identified as a gap among LGBTQI activists. When asked whether a mechanism exists in Italy to bridge and facilitate the communications between LGBTQI organizations and multi-sector stakeholders, Lucia Urciuoli, Communication and Fundraising Expert at Edge, reported that this has become a top priority of her organization. While Edge does not have the mandate and capacity to carry forward the work that actors are doing on the ground, the organization intends to become a platform where demand and supply meet, and mutually beneficial partnerships between companies and non-profits can be forged. This linking role will be extremely beneficial. To ensure the sustainability and accountability of partners' relationships, capacity-building opportunities for fundraising communications, planning and management will also have to be created.

Major findings on media making and digital artifacts of political engagement

Digital media are important tools for disenfranchised people to gain a voice, advance counter-narratives and advocate for social change beyond the boundaries of mainstream corporate media. Whether it is the planning of a political campaign, lobbying, organizing a demonstration or rally, coordinating social movement mobilizations online and offline, or creating media and digital storytelling to promote events, raising awareness about issues, struggles and experiences, communication is central to both activism and resistance. Nevertheless, without falling into technological determinism or over-romanticizing the wonders of the media, it is important to highlight that technology alone will not be enough to promote successful activism and empowerment. Language matters and the way activists construct and craft their narratives will have an impact on whether digital media can truly become tools for radical social change.

The multi-site situational analysis that was conducted in the first stages of this research brought to light several powerful digital artifacts of political engagement produced by LGBTQI actors that were worth analyzing. These included: self-made short campaign videos streamed on social media during National Coming Out Day celebrations; documentary films investigating parents' point of view and reactions to their children's coming out, as well as zooming into LGBT people's everyday lives; positive self-representations of transgender people in web series; a campaign video using the power of emotion and activism to advocate for Rainbow Families' rights; a short film advocating for same-sex marriage and equal rights; queer webcomics and a web-reportage.

The analysis of these digital artifacts of political engagement has provided valuable insights into how semiotic resources have been used to challenge prevailing sociocultural beliefs, stereotypes, prejudices and norms. Rather than opting for a confrontational approach, the digital media activism that is being championed by Italian LGBTQI activists is one targeted toward educating the public about the human rights issues at stake, establishing an emotional connection to the cause, encouraging people to take action and change their behavior. Furthermore, these analyses brought to the surface the shifts in actors' rhetorical activism from early messaging, narratives and discourses mainly focused on awareness-raising of human-rights abuses, suffering and grief, to a more empowering contemporary rhetorical activism expressed through digital media cultures. In a context where the Italian mainstream media continue to contextualize LGBTQI stories using the frames of crime and violence, through their digital media activism, actors have adopted a "peace lens" in their communications. Instead of emphasizing the "negatives," how the country is lagging behind when it comes to the promotion and protection of LGBTQI rights, its failure to prevent and counteract homo/transphobia and misogyny, more emancipatory stories are being told about human rights defenders, politicians who are standing up for

LGBTQI people, and community members who are fully integrated and accepted into society.

Media literacy: a response to current digital divides

Digital media tools and access to the Internet are becoming available to most of the Italian population. As mentioned earlier, 41 million Italians are active on social media (Kemp, 2021), with Italy ranking sixth in Europe for its average daily social media use (Tankovska, 2021). Yet, digital divides still exist, particularly across territorial grassroots periphery realities. These include:

- *Age*: Inequalities in media use, production and access are experienced by different age groups in the population, for instance, digital natives (generally born after the 1980s) vs. digital immigrants (those born before 1980s).
- *Socio-economic status*: Privileged segments of LGBT communities are more likely to hold decision-making positions and shape advocacy agendas.
- *Language*: Prominence of English vs. Italian digital contents concerning LGBTQI community thematic issues, including research, studies, publications, campaigns, case studies, among others.
- *Access to skills*: Lack of capacity building programs on organizational communication strategies, digital media activism, social media marketing, fundraising and grant proposal writing, media production, among others.
- *Distribution of resources*: Larger cities are exposed to greater opportunities and funding compared to smaller cities and territorial municipalities.
- *Media literacy skills*: The abilities to: access information about our communities and the world; analyze how issues are being represented in the media; evaluate the perspectives that are missing and overlooked; and create and distribute messages through different media formats, increasing public dialogue on issues that matter and creating new avenues for alternative representations (Share and Thoman, 2007), are essential to digital media activism, transmedia organizing and active citizenship. Mastering these critical analysis and production skills is a top priority for LGBTQI actors to reclaim their authentic voices across multiple media platforms, organize, mobilize and promote human rights, and overcome many of the challenges identified earlier in this chapter.

Major findings on legislation, restorative justice measures and public opinion

This research has also been invested in unpacking whether the implementation of Law 76/2016 on civil unions has had any effect on public opinion (mainly online, but also offline). The highly mediated nature of the debates that took place in Italy prior to and after the enactment of Law 76/2016, as well as initiatives such as the maps of intolerance, produced by the Vox Observatory on Human Rights, have provided valuable insights into the positions taken by the Italian population toward LGBTQI people and their rights. For some, the law on civil unions is considered a historic step forward and arguably also a catalyst for positive change in Italians' public attitudes toward homosexuals. However, even if the latter includes several provisions from civil marriage, the ongoing tensions between lesbian and gay couples' expectations of equality and, on the other hand, the insistence of separating same-sex civil unions from civil marriage, still risks reinforcing forms of discrimination on the basis of sexual orientation and relegating homosexuals to a status of inferiority.

During the interviews conducted with key actors, there was a general consensus that it may be too soon to assess whether a real change in public attitudes has taken place after the enactment of Law 76/2016. Nevertheless, consistent with Flores and Barclay's (2016) legitimacy model and Aksoy et al.'s (2018) evidence from same-sex relationship recognition policies in Europe, also this research has shown that laws, as well as the initiatives and campaigns spearheaded by a stronger and more unified LGBTQI Italian movement in the years leading up to the passing of the civil union law, notably have contributed to shaping public consciousness and promoting more favorable attitudes and perceptions toward the LGBTQI community. The enactment of the law, increased visibility and representations of the LGBT community, including in mainstream media, and educational and awareness raising programs played a key role in promoting a cultural shift and diminishing online hate. However, enforcing laws is just one step forward.

Changing people's attitudes and behaviors and ultimately attaining positive peace will require a deep transformation in both the institutions and the discourses that reproduce violence. Counteraction, strengthening institutional systems to combat hate speech and hate crime, policies on social inclusion, restorative justice measures, reconciliation efforts and promoting a culture of human rights are critical and necessary to eradicate and heal hate. As shown earlier, in the past two decades, Italy has experienced a significant rise in the number of recorded episodes of hate crime and incitement to hatred against individuals based on ethnic, racial, religious, and sexual grounds. In spite of national and international existing laws, policies and regulatory frameworks in place, the country has also witnessed an increasing number of homotransphobic acts, as reported by many LGBTQI organizations. The absence of a law that would protect people from homotransphobia leads to under-reporting and under-recording of homotransphobic violent acts, pushing further away the prospects of peace, justice, equality and security.

During the time this research was conducted, the advocacy priorities and discourses of the Italian LGBTQI social movement have shifted and these could not be ignored. The advocacy that has taken place during the years leading to the passing of the law on civil unions is now greatly inspiring the digital media activism practices that the democratic party is using to advocate for the passing of the Zan Bill to prevent and combat discrimination and violence on the grounds of sex, gender, sexual orientation, gender identity and disability. This bill predisposes harsher penalties for hate perpetrators and is being widely opposed by a minority of right-wing parties, the Roman Catholic Church, conservative anti-gender groups, and radical and trans-exclusionary feminists. Transcending prejudice, misconceptions and fears and fully realizing that what LGBTQI people want is equal rights and not special rights are important. A hope for the near future is that Italians will be fully aware that the recently rejected Zan Bill is an opportunity the country cannot miss to have in place a legal framework tackling both retributive and restorative justice measures that will enable institutions to better protect the most vulnerable victims of discrimination, intolerance and homotransphobia.

Avenues for future research

Italian mass media and the entertainment industry have greatly contributed to shaping the ways in which Italians understand and learn about the LGBTQI community. Yet, representations of LGBTQI subjectivities and gender identities in the popular culture discourses have been greatly overlooked and underexplored by Italian scholars, with the exception of several initiatives such as the Diversity Media Awards launched in Italy in 2016 and modeled after the GLAAD Media Awards. In collaboration with universities and think tanks in Italy, Diversity (the organization spearheading this initiative), conducts quantitative and qualitative research assessing and acknowledging fair, accurate, and diverse representations of LGBTQI people in the Italian media, including television, radio and cinema. However, the existing research gaps in the field of LGBTQI media culture in Italy deserve greater attention since it is precisely these mainstream representations that have contributed in most cases to the dissemination of distorted harmful narratives about LGBTQI people, fueling negative stereotyping, increasing prejudices, hate, discrimination and homophobia, also leading to direct physical violence in many cases. Creating authentic self-representations of LGBTQI individuals and mainstreaming empowering non-violent narratives are imperative in attempts to educate the public, create a culture of respect and non-discrimination, and encourage action and behavioral change. Yet, as shown in this book, these authentic and positive representations often find their place in more peripherical online spaces outside the domain of traditional mainstream media.

In a context where the voices of LGBTQI activists are still often marginalized and silenced in both political and public discourses, online and offline, reclaiming activists' voices and bringing to light their cultural resistance practices have been one of the key aims of this book. The trigger for investigating their contentious politics expressed through digital media activism was driven by the strong belief that when counter-hate discourses and coping mechanisms are symbolically annihilated and rendered invisible, also human rights abuses and violations risk being neglected and under-reported. Taking an intersectional approach to the study of social movements and digital media activism and using a human rights, peace and conflict framework in this endeavor have greatly strengthened this work. However, in the study of the extensive literature on communications, media and social movements studies, it was evident that scholars coming from diverse academic disciplines employ very different approaches to studying, understanding and theorizing about the transformative effects of digital media in social movements dynamics. For instance, social scientists and media scholars may lack extensive knowledge of human rights mechanisms and standards, as well as peace and conflict management strategies. The latter could greatly strengthen research outcomes of the social movements and media activism dynamics. At the same time, political scientists, human rights and peace and conflict scholars may not have a strong background in the field of social, cultural and critical media studies, digital media, social networks and contemporary visual cultures, political communications, among others. A more intersectional and interdisciplinary approach to the study of social movements and media activism dynamics is required.

This work has also shed light on the online mobilizations and protest action that are increasingly replacing street protests and offline activism, particularly since the start of the COVID-19 pandemic. By acknowledging existing digital divides, further avenues for research may involve studying the relationship and interdependence of online and offline activism, and how these complement each other when protecting and promoting human rights and advancing political claims. Furthermore, it will be worth exploring why Italian LGBTQI youth activists are not engaging as much in offline participatory action. Why are organizations struggling to recruit new supporters and allies on the ground? Are incentives missing or are organizations and institutions failing to communicate the case for advocacy and activism? In addition, are traditional activism cultures, visions and approaches too stuck in the past? These are some of the questions worth asking when advancing research on social movements and digital media activism.

Finally, while most scholars have turned their attention to the study of anti-gender movements and their hegemonic and harmful discourses (which are also the most prominent in news media and television), this research wanted to redirect the spotlight onto the peaceful, non-violent and emancipatory narratives of LGBTQI actors expressed through their digital artifacts of political engagement. Currently, very limited academic research exists on this topic. Italian activists' cultural resistance work is seldom acknowledged, seen or heard, not only by politicians and the general population, but also by LGBTQI activists themselves who belong to different organizations and geographic locations. Scholarship on peace communication and counter-hate speech produced by peace and conflict analysts has mostly addressed mainstream journalism, missing the opportunity to reach out to a great number of activists and communication practitioners in the search for effective non-violent strategies to respond to conflict and improve the prospects of peace, justice and equality. Future research focusing on the production and analysis of peaceful and counter-hate media artifacts of political engagement is greatly encouraged in order to amplify the voices and existence of those standing on the margins and the most vulnerable victims of discrimination and human rights violations.

References

Askoy, C.G., Carpenter, >C.S., De Haas, R., and Tran, K. (2018) Do laws shape attitudes? Evidence from same-sex relationship recognition policies in Europe, IZA Institute of Labor Economics. Available at: http://ftp.iza.org/dp11743.pdf.

Flores, A.R., and Barclay, S. (2016). Backlash, consensus, legitimacy, or polarization: The effect of same-sex marriage policy on mass attitudes, *Political Research Quarterly*, 69 (1), 43–56.

Kemp, S. (2021) Digital 2021: Italy. Available at: www.datareportal.com.

Share, J., and Thoman, E. (2007) *Teaching Democracy: A Media Literacy Approach*, Los Angeles, CA: The National Center for the Preservation of Democracy.

Tankovska, H. (2021) Average daily social media use in selected European countries 2020, Statista. Available at: https://www.statista.com/statistics/719966/average-daily-social-media-use-in-selected-european-countries

Index

www.ingramcontent.com/pod-product-compliance
Ingram Content Group UK Ltd.
Pitfield, Milton Keynes, MK11 3LW, UK
UKHW020416010325
455677UK00029B/912